Quick & Easy

DONBURI DISHES

Healthy Rice Bowl Toppings

OVERSEAS DISTRIBUTORS

UNITED STATES: JP TRADING, INC.
      400 Forbes Blvd., Unit 3
      South San Francisco, CA 94080
      Phone: (650) 871-3940
      Fax: (650) 871-3944
U.S.A.: A.K. HARANO COMPANY
U.S.A.: MASA T. & ASSOCIATES
HAWAII: HAKUBUNDO, INC.
GUAM, SAIPAN AND MICRONESIAN ISLANDS: FUJIWARA'S SALES AND SERVICE
CANADA: MILESTONE PUBLICATIONS
MEXICO: EDITORIAL SAYROLS, S.A. DE C.V.
COLOMBIA: JORGE E. MORALES & CIA. LTDA.
SINGAPORE: MPH DISTRIBUTORS (S) PTE. LTD.
MALAYSIA: MPH DISTRIBUTORS SDN, BHD.
PHILIPPINES: NATIONAL BOOK STORE, INC.
INDONESIA: TOKO BUKU HARAPAN
INDIA: DANI BOOK LAND, Mumbai (Bombay) 14
AUSTRALIA: BOOKWISE INTERNATIONAL
THAILAND: CENTRAL BOOKS DISTRIBUTION, LTD.
KOREA: TONGJIN CHULPAN MUYEOK CO., LTD.
TAIWAN: FORMOSAN MAGAZINE PRESS, LTD.
HONG KONG: APOLLO BOOK COMPANY, LTD.

Original copyright © 2000 by Boutique-sha

World rights reserved. Published by Joie, Inc. 1-8-3, Hirakawa-cho, Chiyoda-ku, Tokyo 102-0093 Japan.   Printed in Japan

ISBN4-915831-91-4

CONTENTS

DONBURI—A WELL-BALANCED, FAST MEAL 4

DONBURI COOKING TIPS 5

RICE AND RICE COOKING 6

GLOSSARY 7

SASHIMI DONBURI 10

AUTHENTIC DONBURI 20

LIGHT AND HEALTHY DONBURI 28

NOURISHING DONBURI 36

POWER DONBURI 46

SPICY DONBURI 52

SPECIAL DINNER DONBURI 58

EASY DONBURI 64

COLORFUL DONBURI FOR KIDS 70

LOW CALORIE DONBURI 76

CALCIUM-RICH SEAFOOD DONBURI 82

INDEX 89

BASIC MEASUREMENTS 92

DONBURI—A WELL-BALANCED, FAST MEAL

The word "*donburi*" may not sound as familiar as *sushi*, *teriyaki*, or some other well-known Japanese dishes. *Donburi* literally refers to the large, thick rice bowl that often comes with a lid. However, it is also what the Japanese call a meal of rice with some sort of topping, served in a bowl. Various toppings and condiments can be served over steaming hot rice, usually with a savory sauce seeping in. This all-in-one meal has always been popular because it includes everything in one deep bowl, saving time in preparation and cleanup.

The idea parallels that of the American casserole or sandwich, in which all of the ingredients are combined with or without a sauce to make a healthy meal in just one container or bite-size pieces. The plain taste of rice is enhanced by the toppings just like bread is in the West.

Thus *donburi-mono*, or *donburi* dishes, fits easily into today's lifestyle of the Japanese and *donburi* lunchrooms have sprouted everywhere in the country, just as numerous as the hamburger chainstores. One successful *donburi* chain expanded by leaps and bounds with the catchphrase, "*hayai*, *yasui*, *umai*", meaning quick, reasonable, and delicious.

Donburi has always been a homestyle food. So it is interesting to find that Japanese restaurants list the prices of such dishes according to the containers they are served in, e.g. lacquered box and *donburi* bowl. On a menu, you will find *tempura*-and-rice dish in two styles, *ten-juu*(lacquered box) and *ten-don*(bowl). As you might have guessed, *ten-don* always costs less. It is just a polite way of indicating the price while avoiding such expressions as "fine" grade and "regular" grade. Popular *donburi* can be shortened to "*don*" when added to the name of the topping, like *gyu-don* for beef *donburi*, or *ten-don* for *tempura donburi*. Other "coined" ones are named "so-and-so" *donburi* like *yakitori donburi*.

By using toppings ranging from costly *ikura* to more economical chicken-and-eggs, there are endless variations of *donburi*. You can create balanced, nutritional and flavorful *donburi* dishes to suit the tastes of your family. We hope this book will encourage you to try to make your own examples of this healthy dish from Japan.

DONBURI COOKING TIPS

Most toppings in this book can be cooked in a single frying pan. Use the smallest one on hand for the best results. You don't have to purchase *donburi* bowls described below. Substitute with soup bowls, deep salad or cereal bowls.

Donburi bowls

A standard *donburi* measures 6"(15cm) in diameter, 3 ½"(9cm) deep, and holds about 1½ cups of cooked rice. Children's sizes are also available. It comes with a matching lid to keep the food warm. Besides, it is fun to anticipate what might be inside your bowl as you uncover it.

Types of topping

Donburi toppings can be sorted into four types according to the method of cooking: Fresh, simmered, fried, and grilled.

Simmered or braised toppings are most common, including the ones that are bound with softly beaten eggs. This type of topping is quickly prepared and eaten with the thickened cooking sauce poured over plain rice. This type includes BEEF BOWL (*gyu-don*), CHICKEN-AND-EGG DONBURI (*oyako-don*), CLAM DONBURI (Fukagawa-*don*).

Uncooked toppings are usually seafood such as *sashimi* and fish eggs. Rice is often seasoned with sweet vinegar, just like *sushi* base. When selecting seafood, take the freshest ones that spring back to the touch, and slice them just before serving. This type of *donburi* includes SALMON ROE DONBURI (*ikura-don*), SEA URCHIN DONBURI (*uni-don*), and *MAGURO SASHIMI* DONBURI (*tekka-don*).

Fried toppings are usually served with a sauce poured over them. Crisp coating absorbs the rich sauce which also seasons the plain rice, making a distinctive harmony in your mouth. This type includes PORK CUTLET DONBURI (*katsu-don*), and *TEMPURA* DONBURI (*ten-don*).

Grilled toppings such as *teriyaki* eel, chicken, or steak also need matching sauces that are prepared separately. The trick to this type of topping is to grill the meat or fish until browned and aromatic like when barbecuing. Also, cut the topping into bite sized pieces before arranging on the rice. *YAKITORI* DONBURI and GRILLED SQUID DONBURI are the typical examples of this kind.

Hints for the best donburi

1. Be sure to cut or slice the ingredients so they can be cooked fast. The cooking sauce may scorch by the time a lump of meat cooks completely, causing a change in the flavor.

2. It is recommendable to warm *donburi* bowls by filling them with hot water until the moment you put the rice in.

3. Fill the bowl half to ¾ full with cooked rice, leaving enough room for the topping. 1 serving of rice is about 1½ cups in cooked form. Be sure to load the bowl with fluffed rice without pressing down or packing it tightly.

4. When making a topping that is bound together with eggs, it is best to cook one portion at a time , using a small, shallow frying pan for easy handling. Barely cooked, succulent eggs may be torn apart when being transferred onto rice. In Japan a tiny, shallow pan called *oyako-nabe,* made specially for this purpose, is commonly used.

RICE AND RICE COOKING

Short or medium grain, white rice is used in Japanese cuisine.

In this book, recipes exclude how to cook the rice since every dish needs cooked rice, hot or cool. Always prepare rice first, and while it is being cooked, make the topping.

Allow 30-60 minutes for preparation of rice including washing and soaking time. (Rice can be prepared in a large batch days ahead, then refrigerated or frozen to be microwaved just before serving. Be sure to reheat until piping hot.) Some rice is available prewashed which would save the washing process. The taste is just as good.

An automatic, electric rice cooker (see below for automatic cooking) does a perfect job especially for cooking a large amount like 5 cups, but if not available to you, follow the steps below. A Dutch oven or a heavy-bottomed saucepan with a fitted lid should work as well.

Washing

1. In a bowl or pot, place measured rice. Pour in water just to cover, and gently stir with your hand. Discard milky water.

2. Add fresh water and stir well, pressing the rice with the palm of your hand. Discard white water. Repeat 3-4 times until the water is almost clear; drain.

3. Soak rice in fresh water. Add 1-1⅙ cups water per each cup of rice. If using rice that has been on the shelf for over 6 months, increase to 1⅓ water each. Let stand for 30 minutes for the best result.

Cooking

4. Do not discard the water, and place the pot on stove. Bring to a boil over low to medium heat and cook for 10 minutes, gradually raising the heat to high. (Adjust the heat as necessary to make sure the water does not boil over.)

5. Keep boiling for 1 minute over high heat.

6. Reduce the heat to very low and simmer for a further 10-12 minutes.

7. Remove from heat and let stand, covered, for 10-15 minutes. This steaming process is essential for the grains to absorb the moisture. Do not remove the lid during this final cooking.

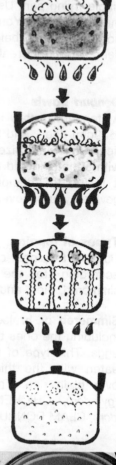

8. After steaming, fluff cooked rice in the pot, with a dampened rice paddle so as to introduce air. This way, the rice will keep the best flavor longer.

Notes for automatic rice cooker users

Electric rice cooker with a timer saves your time and effort considerably. All you have to do is wash rice and put into the inner pot, adding water to the indicated line. It does the heat adjustments automatically and keeps the rice hot until needed. You can even set the timer hours ahead. Just be careful about the rice measuring. A Japanese cup measures 200ml while an American cup holds 240ml, and 250ml in an Australian cup. Read the manual carefully, and use the attached measuring cup for rice.

GLOSSARY

Abura-age —Thin fried *tofu*. This fluffy type fried *tofu* is mainly used for simmered dishes since the crisp outside absorbs flavors than regular *tofu*. It is often added to *miso* soups, and also is made into pouches for *inari-zushi*, a vegetarian *sushi*.

Atsu-age —Thick fried *tofu* with less moisture than regular *tofu*. It is grilled or simmered just like the thin type.

Atsuyaki tamago —Thick omelet, usually seasoned with sugar, salt and *sake*.

Chirimenjako —Dried baby sardine which are lightly salted.

Cucumber —Japanese-type cucumbers are smaller in size and have tenderer skin and less seeds. No peeling or seeding is necessary.

Daikon radish —Large white radish, 10"-20"(25-50 cm) long, 3"-4"(7.5-10cm) thick. This radish is a must for Japanese tables and is eaten in numerous ways such as pickling, frying, and simmering, besides being grated to make condiments.

Dashi —A basic stock widely used in Japanese cooking. *Kombu*(giant kelp) and dried bonito flakes are cooked briefly in boiling water, and then removed to make a clear broth. Today busy wives prefer using powdered or granulated form which are availabie in jars or sachets.

Dashimaki tamago —Thick omelet. Often confused with *atsuyaki tamago*, but this type includes *dashi* stock in the egg mixture, therefore the texture is tenderer and the taste is milder.

Eggplant —Japanese type eggplant is smaller in size and has tenderer texture and skin. Be careful about the amount if using western type.

Enokidake mushroom —Whitish mushroom with tiny caps and long, narrow stems, cultivated in the same condition as the common button mushrooms. They have a delicate flavor and pleasant crispness.

Ginger root —Ginger is used only in fresh form in Asian cooking. Look for firm rhizomes when choosing.

Gomokuzushi-no-moto —A convenient mix of sea- soned ingredients for making *sushi* melange (mixed *sushi*) at home. Available in jar or pouches.

Ikura —Salted salmon roe, treasured highly just as western caviar. It makes a popular topping for *sushi*.

Kabayaki —*Kabayaki* stands for fish fillets grilled with *teriyaki* sauce. The sauce is sold as *kabayaki-no-tare*.

Kamaboko —Fish cake. White meat fish paste is heaped on a piece of wood, and steamed to make a resilient, savory cake.

Kezuribushi —Shavings of smoked-and-dried bonito now sold in small pouches. The main ingredient for *dashi* stock, but is also used as a garnish or topping to add flavor to various Japanese dishes.

Kinome —Sprout of *sansho*, or Japanese pepper, which releases a strong fragrance and makes a decorative garnish for the springtime dishes.

Kochu jang —Korean hot sauce made from barley and soy bean malts. Comes in a jar and keeps indefinitely if refrigerated.

Konnyaku —Sold as "yam cake", this is a jelly made of cooked gelatinous mountain yam. It became popular in Japan also as a health food because it contains no calories but lots of dietary fiber.

Long onion —*Naganegi* or Tokyo *negi*. Thick, long onion used widely in Asian cooking. Looks similar to leek, but its flavor resembles spring onion or green onion.

Mentaiko —Chili-flavored, heavily salted cod roe. It has become very popular in Japan since the introduction from Korea, and is served as a part of everyday meal. Other than being eaten on its own, it also makes great dressings for seafood or vegetable salads.

Mentsuyu —*Sobatsuyu*, or *soba* soup base. Bottled *mentsuyu* is available in Japanese food section. It can be used as a cooking sauce for simmered foods. Adjust the amount of soy sauce and salt when doing so.

Mirin —A thick, sweet wine made from rice, used primarily in cooking. It gives rich flavor and glaze to food such as *teriyaki*. If not in hand, substitute with *sake* and sugar, in a ratio of 2 : 1.

Miso —Fermented soybean paste. It is a must-have seasoning in most households in Japan. Besides being used for making *miso* soups and dressings, it is used as a pickling bed or a dip. There are numerous types including yellow, brown and dark brown in color, and sweet to salty in flavor.

Mitsuba —Trefoil, a member of the parsley family. This herb has a delicate fragrance, somewhere between sorrel and celery, and is used to accent many Japanese dishes.

Myoga —Young, pinkish fresh ginger flower head, treasured as a special summer herb. It has a distinctive fragrance which enhances various salads, soups and pickles. Also good for *tempura* or pickling.

Nakaochi —Paste-like *maguro sashimi*, scooped out from between tuna bones. Loved for its fatty flavor and often served in rolled *sushi* rolls.

Nameko mushroom —Tiny, yellow to reddish brown mushroom with glutenous cap. The jelly-like substance that covers the brown cap is said to protect the walls of your stomach from strong acid or salt irritation. However, *nameko* mushroom has been loved for its smooth touch and delicate flavor, rather than for its health effect. Available in cans or bags.

Nametake —*Enokidake* mushrooms boiled down with soy sauce and other seasonings are called "*nametake*", and is convenient for everyday cooking. Available in jars.

Natto —Fermented soybeans with a sticky texture and strong aroma. Some westerners may take some time to acquire the taste. It is a great source of protein and vitamin K, and usually served with scallion and hot mustard.

Nikujaga —One of the best selling small dishes in *Izakaya* Japanese pubs. *Niku* (meat) and *jaga* (potatoes) are simmered in sweet-salty sauce.

Nira —Garlic chives. A flat, fleshy and soft vegetable with a strong garlic flavor. Added to egg dishes, dim sums and soups.

Nori seaweed —Known as a wrapper for *sushi*, this edible blackish seaweed comes in dried, thin sheets. Needs to be stored in an airtight container.

Nozawana —Giant greens from Nozawa district in Nagano. Known widely as a light pickle which is refreshing and crunchy.

Pickled ginger —*Beni-shoga*. Fresh ginger pickled in sweet vinegar, often colored in pink or red and served as a garnish.

Rice vinegar —This vinegar has a milder flavor than most western vinegars. Its lightness and subtle sweetness are essential for seasoning cooked rice for *sushi* or dressings for Japanese style salads.

Sake —Rice wine. Known as a popular Japanese beverage, *sake* also plays a major role in Japanese cooking. It is used to remove unpleasant odors of meat or fish, and to soften meat or vegetables quickly, as well as to give a delicate flavor to most dishes. Once opened, *sake* should be kept in a cool, dark place just like wines.

Sansai —Mixed wild plants. Usually sold as a ready-to-use mix of precooked ferns, young bamboo shoots, mushrooms and sometimes *konnyaku*, packed in plastic bags.

Sansho —Japanese pepper. Powdered form of *sansho* fruit, used as a spice.

Sashimi —Sliced fresh fish served "au naturel". *Maguro sashimi* is most popular, but any fresh fish including shellfish can be called *sashimi*. Chilled and served with soy sauce and *wasabi*, or sometimes grated ginger.

Sesame oil —An essential, fragrant oil used in Asian cooking. Sesame oil has a nutty flavor and is mainly added for flavoring food rather than for cooking.

7-spice powder —An aromatic ready-mix of seven Japanese spices: red pepper, *sansho* pepper, green *nori* seaweed, white sesame seeds, citrus peel, linen seeds and poppy seeds.

Shiba-zuke —Well-known pickle originated in Kyoto. Cucumbers and eggplant are salted and then vinegar-pickled with red *shiso* leaves and *myoga* sprouts to give fragrance and pleasant color.

Shiitake mushroom —A large, dark brown mushroom used in both fresh and dried forms. It has a distinctive aroma and smoothness, and is used in many Japanese dishes. The best way of softening dried *shiitake* is: Soak in water with a pinch of sugar and refrigerate for an hour.

Shimeji mushroom — A greyish white mushroom that grows with overlapping oyster-shell-shaped caps.

Shirataki —Sold as "yam noodles", opaque filaments made from *konnyaku* yam. *Shirataki* is a must for *sukiyaki* because it absorbs flavors well and the texture is smooth and slippery. Parboiling is often necessary to remove a lime substance.

Shiso —Perilla leaves in green or purple-red color. This herb is related to the mint family and has a pleasant aroma. Green *shiso* is mainly used for cooking or as a condiment for *sashimi* platters while red *shiso* is often added to pickled vegetables.

Soy sauce —A salty, dark-brown colored sauce made by fermenting soy beans in brine. Choose clear-colored product. Once opened soy sauce doesn't keep many months, and should be kept in cool, dark place.

Sukiyaki —Popular one-pot dish of thinly sliced beef, *tofu* and vegetables boiled down with *sake*, soy sauce and sugar. When cooking, each ingredients are kept separately, and not stirred. See page 39 for more details.

Sudachi citron —A tiny green citron with refreshing fragrance resembling lime.

Takuan —Pickled *daikon* radish, yellow or whitish in color. *Takuan* is loved for its crispness and is readily available in plastic bags.

Tarako —Codfish roe, usually salted for preserving purpose. *Tarako* is one of the most popular salted fish eggs as well as *ikura*, which is favored like caviar.

Tempura —Seafood or vegetable coated in a light batter and deep-fried in oil. The temperature of oil should be kept right for crisp *tempura*.

Toban jang —Chinese seasoning known as hot bean paste. It is made from soy beans, chili peppers and sometimes garlic. Comes in jars or cans.

Tofu —Soybean curd. *Tofu* is rich in proteins, vitamins and minerals, and is entirely free of cholesterol because of the low content of saturated fat. *Tofu* cakes should be kept in water, which should be changed daily.

Umeboshi —Pickled Japanese plum. *Umeboshi* is a traditional health food of Japan, and has long been used as a tonic, not only because it helps digestion but also keeps the intestinal tract clear. *Umeboshi* paste makes a piquant dressing for seafood salads and is available in tubes.

Uni —Sea urchin roe, usually served fresh as *sushi* or *sashimi*. Cooked *uni* seasoned with *sake* is called *neri-uni* and is available in jars. It is convenient to be used as a base of sauces for various food.

Yakitori —Popular appetizer dish. Bite-sized chicken pieces on bamboo skewers are grilled over direct heat, preferably on charcoal, and glazed with *teriyaki* sauce. Chicken balls, livers and even beef pieces are called *yakitori* as long as they are cooked in the same method.

Yama-imo —Mountain yam favored for its glutenous, smooth texture and nutritious value. To prevent discoloring, *yama-imo* is soaked a little while in vinegared water after it is peeled.

Wasabi —Japanese green horseradish, most familiar in the west as a mound of pungent green paste served with *sushi* and *sashimi*. Originally, the rhizome is grated finely, however, nowadays *wasabi* is available in tubes or small pouches. It has been proved that *wasabi* has sterilizing properties.

SASHIMI DONBURI

CONTENTS

SALMON ROE DONBURI p.11
SEA URCHIN DONBURI p.11
MIXED *MAGURO* DONBURI p.12
MAGURO SASHIMI DONBURI
                        p.12
MASHED *MAGURO* DONBURI
                        p.13
SQUID AND COD ROE DONBURI
                        p.14
MARINATED SQUID DONBURI
                        p.14
SQUID AND *NATTO* DONBURI
                        p.15
OCTOPUS DONBURI p.15
ASSORTED *SASHIMI* DONBURI
                        p.16
SCALLOP DONBURI p.16
TROUGH SHELL SCALLOP DONBURI
                        p.17
SALMON *OYAKO* DONBURI p.18
CRAB *OYAKO* DONBURI p.19
CODFISH *OYAKO* DONBURI p.19

In most districts along the seas, the day's fresh takes were placed over hot rice, to be enjoyed immediately. This feast which was envied by the people living inland is no more only a fishermen's privilege. Select the freshest fish carefully, cut them into bite-size pieces just before serving. Enjoy these healthy, oil-free dishes, oops, bowls!

SALMON ROE DONBURI *(Ikura-don)*

3-4 cups hot cooked rice (see p.6)
2 oz (60g) *ikura* (salted salmon roe)
MARINADE
⅔ cup *dashi* stock
1 Tbsp *sake*
1 Tbsp soy sauce
1 Tbsp light soy sauce
1 small bunch *mitsuba* (trefoil)
2 tsp toasted white sesame seeds

Serves: 2

1 Make marinade. In a small saucepan, bring *dashi* stock to a boil, add *sake* and reheat to release alcohol. Add soy sauces; remove from heat.

2 Transfer marinade into a container and let stand to cool. When completely cooled, add *ikura* and set aside about 30 minutes.

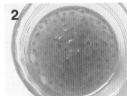

3 Blanch *mitsuba* in boiling water for 3-4 seconds, and cut into 1"(2.5cm) lengths.

4 Toss rice with sesame seeds and *mitsuba* using a spatula. Do not break grains. Place in each serving bowl and top with drained *ikura*.

SEA URCHIN DONBURI *(Uni-don)*

3-4 cups hot cooked rice (see p.6)
2 oz (60 g) fresh sea urchin (*uni*)
½ sheet *nori* seaweed
Dash *wasabi* paste
Soy sauce for dip

Serves: 2

1 Cut *nori* seaweed into fine strips, using kitchen scissors.

2 In each serving bowl, place hot cooked rice. Scatter with *nori* strips.

3 Top rice with sea urchin and *wasabi* paste. Serve with soy sauce.

Hint: Substitute with *sushi* rice for plain hot one, for a change. See page 12 for *sushi* rice recipe.

MIXED *MAGURO* DONBURI
(*Maguro Tekone-zushi Donburi*)

3-4 cups *sushi* rice (see below)
5 oz (150g) *maguro sashimi*
⌈2½ Tbsp soy sauce
⌊1 Tbsp *sake*
1 Tbsp toasted white sesame seeds
5-6 stalks chives or scalion

Serves: 2

1 Make *sushi* rice referring **How to Make Sushi Rice** (below).

2 Cut *maguro sashimi* into small, bite-size pieces. Place in a small bowl and pour over soy sauce and *sake*; set aside and chop chives.

3 Drain *maguro* pieces and toss lightly with cooled *sushi* rice, using your hand. Do not stir.

4 Place in a bowl and sprinkle with chives and sesame seeds.

How to Make *Sushi* Rice

3 cups hot cooked rice (see p.6)
SUSHI VINEGAR
⌈2½ Tbsp rice vinegar
|1½ Tbsp sugar
⌊¾ tsp salt
Makes: 3 cups

1 In a small bowl, put *SUSHI* VINEGAR ingredients and stir well until the sugar and salt are completely dissolved.
2 In a medium bowl, place steaming cooked rice (microwave if using cold rice), and pour *sushi* vinegar over it, distributing it around the bowl evenly. Using a spatula, fluff rice evenly so as not to break the grains. When the vinegar blends in, cool immediately, using a fan.

Hint: For the best flavor, place a small piece of *kombu* kelp on rice when cooking.

MAGURO SASHIMI DONBURI
(*Tekka-don*)

3-4 cups *sushi* rice (see above)
3½oz (100g) *maguro sashimi*
⌈2 Tbsp soy sauce
⌊1 Tbsp *sake*
½ sheet *nori* seaweed
Dash grated *daikon* radish, optional
Dash *wasabi* paste, optinal

Serves: 2

1 Marinate sliced *maguro sashimi* in soy sauce and *sake* overnight.

2 Put *nori* seaweed in a plastic bag and crumble into pieces.

3 Place *sushi* rice in each serving bowl, and cover with *nori*. Arrange *maguro* slices and garnish with grated *radish* and/or *wasabi* paste.

Note: Leftover *sashimi* can be greatly enhanced with this method.

MASHED *MAGURO* DONBURI *(Negitoro-don)*

3-4 cups hot cooked rice (see p.6)
4 oz(120g) *nakaochi* of fresh *maguro*
2 Tbsp soy sauce
2 tsp *sake*
Few stalks chives or scallion
Half dozen *shiso*(perilla) leaves
Dash *wasabi* paste

Serves: 2

Note: *Nakaochi* is irregular shaped bits of *maguro sashimi*, scooped out from the bony center of tuna. It attracts gourmets' taste buds because of the rich flavor.

1 In a bowl, place *maguro sashimi* bits. Chop *maguro* if large pieces are included.

2 Chop chives and add to *maguro*. Pour in soy sauce and *sake*. Mix lightly so the seasonings penetrate evenly.

3 Place hot cooked rice in each serving bowl.

Lay 3 *shiso* leaves each and place *maguro* on them. Garnish with *wasabi* paste. Serve immediately.

SQUID AND COD ROE DONBURI

3-4 cups hot cooked rice (see p.6)
3½-5 oz(100-150g) squid *sashimi*
1 oz(30g) salted chili cod roe (*mentaiko*)
1 tsp *sake*
1 sheet *nori* seaweed

Serves: 2

1 Place skinned cod roe in a small bowl, and sprinkle with *sake*. Add squid strips and mix well.

2 In a plastic bag, put *nori* and break into pieces.

3 Place hot cooked rice in each serving bowl, and scatter *nori*. Mound squid mixture on top.

Hint: By thinning with *sake*, cod roe can be easily mixed with squid.

MARINATED SQUID DONBURI

3-4 cups hot cooked rice (see p.6)
3½-5 oz(100-150g) squid *sashimi*
2"(5 cm) length celery stalk
3 *shiso*(perilla) leaves
2 Tbsp soy sauce

Serves: 2

1 In a small bowl, coat squid *sashimi* with soy sauce.

2 Shave or shred celery using a mandolin or a sharp knife.

3 Shred *shiso* leaves.

4 Place hot cooked rice in each serving bowl, and top with squid, celery and *shiso* leaves.

Hint: Try with other garnish such as spring onion or fresh ginger root.

SQUID AND *NATTO* DONBURI
(*Ika-natto Donburi*)

3-4 cups hot cooked rice (see p.6)
3½-5 oz(100-150g) squid *sashimi*
1¾ oz(50g) *natto* (fermented soybeans)
⎡1 Tbsp soy sauce
½ tsp *mirin*
½ tsp *sake*
⎣Dash hot mustard
1-2 stalks chives or scallion
½ sheet *nori* seaweed
Toasted white sesame seeds

Serves: 2

1 In a bowl, mix *natto* with soy sauce, *mirin*, *sake* and mustard.

2 Slice chives thinly. Using a plastic bag, break *nori* into small pieces.

3 Place hot cooked rice in each serving bowl, place squid *sashimi* to almost cover the rice. Center *natto* mixture.

4 Sprinkle with sesame seeds and *nori*. Garnish with sliced chives.

Hint: Mix everything when eating.

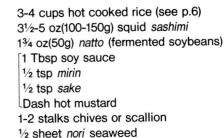

OCTOPUS DONBURI

3-4 cups hot cooked rice (see p.6)
4 oz(120g) boiled octopus tentacle
2 Tbsp soy sauce
1 *sudachi* citron or lime
Chives or scallions
1 knob fresh ginger

Serves: 2

1 Slice octopus tentacle and chives.

2 Shred ginger and soak in cold water 5 minutes; drain.

3 Marinade octopus: In a bowl, blend *sudachi* juice and half amount of soy sauce (1 Tbsp), and toss octopus slices. Let stand about 10 minutes.

4 Place hot cooked rice in each serving bowl. Arrange marinated octopus slices. Sprinkle with chives and remaining soy sauce. Garnish with shredded ginger.

Hint: *Sudachi* and octopus are an excellent combination. 10-minute marinating makes the difference.

15

ASSORTED *SASHIMI* DONBURI *(Kaisen Chirashi Donburi)*

3-4 cups *sushi* rice (see p.12)
6-8 slices *maguro sashimi*
3-4 scallop *sashimi*, sliced
4-6 shrimp *sashimi*
1½ oz (50 g) squid *sashimi*
1½ oz (50 g) trough shell scallops
 (*aoyagi*)
6 slices octopus *sashimi*
4 slices *Dashimaki Tamago* (omelet for
 sushi)
4 slices *kamaboko* (fish cake), optional
 (Red and white slices are used here)
Wasabi paste

Serves: 2

1 Place *sushi* rice in each serving bowl
and arrange *sashimi*, sliced omelet, and
cut-out *kamaboko*. Serve with soy sauce
and *wasabi* paste.

Note: Make an assortment with the
day's freshest *sashimi*. There is no rule
of combination.

How to Make *Dashimaki Tamago*

2 eggs, lightly mixed
⌈2 Tbsp each *dashi* stock, *sake*, sugar
⌊Dash salt
Vegetable oil for greasing
Makes: 1 roll

1 In a small saucepan, bring *dashi* stock, *sake*, sugar and salt to
a boil. Remove from heat and set aside to cool.
2 Blend eggs with *dashi* stock and seasonings, stirring gently to
avoid bubbly texture.
3 Heat a greased, small frying pan or square omelet pan, and
pour ¼ amount of the egg mixture. Cook over very low heat.
Before eggs are set, roll up from one edge. Pour the same
amount of egg mixture onto the surface and roll again. Repeat
until a large rolled omelet is made.
4 Slice the roll into ⅜"(1cm) for topping, 1"(2.5cm) if serving as
appetizer.

SCALLOP DONBURI
(Hotate-don)

3-4 cups *sushi* rice (see p.12)
6 scallop *sashimi*
1 tsp *sake*
4 oz(120g) *yamato-imo* yam
   Few drops vinegar
1½ Tbsp soy sauce
1 *sudachi* citron or lime
4-5 stalks *mitsuba* (trefoil)

Serves: 2

1 Cut scallops into ⅜"(1 cm) cubes, and sprinkle with *sake*; set aside.

2 Peel *yamato-imo* yam and cut likewise, into slightly smaller cubes; soak in vinegared water to remove harshness, about 5 minutes.

3 Blanch *mitsuba* in boiling water for only a few seconds and plunge into cold water. Drain and cut into 1"(2.5 cm) lengths.

4 In a small bowl blend soy sauce and *sudachi* juice. Add scallops and *yamato-imo* yam. Toss well.

5 Place *sushi* rice in each serving bowl, and arrange toppings. Garnish with *mitsuba*.

TROUGH SHELL SCALLOP DONBURI
(Kobashira-don)

3-4 cups *sushi* rice (see p.12)
3 oz (90 g) trough shell scallop (*sashimi*)
1 sheet *nori* seaweed
3-4 *shiso* leaves, shredded
Wasabi paste

Serves: 2

1 In a plastic bag, put *nori* seaweed and "rub" to break into pieces. If *nori* is not dry enough, tear into small pieces.

2 Place *sushi* rice in each serving bowl, and cover the surface with broken *nori* pieces. Center scallops forming a mound, and place shredded *shiso* leaves around it. Serve with *wasabi* and soy sauce.

17

SALMON *OYAKO* DONBURI *(Sake Oyako-don)*

3-4 cups hot cooked rice (see p.6)
4-6 Tbsp salted salmon flakes
1 oz(30 g) *ikura* (salted salmon roe)
5-6 *shiso*(perilla) leaves, shredded

Serves: 2

1 In a large bowl, mix hot cooked rice (cover and microwave if using cold rice) and salmon flakes, gently so as not to break rice grains.

2 Place mixed rice in each serving bowl, and center *ikura*. Arrange shredded *shiso* leaves around it.

Note: Salmon flakes are available in jars. If making from fresh salmon, cook a fillet (about 2½ oz, 70 g) salted salmon and flake it using a fork.

Oyako Donburi

Oyako literally means parent and child, and originally, chicken and eggs on rice are called *oyako-don*. This is a variation using salmon and its eggs.

3-4 cups hot cooked rice (see p.6)
2 oz(60g) canned crab meat
2 Tbsp *kani-no-ko* (salted crab eggs)
1 cup *dashi* stock
1 Tbsp *sake*
1 tsp salt
Red *shiso* seeds, optional

Serves: 2

1 Drain crab meat and remove cartilage.

2 In a small saucepan, bring *dashi* stock, *sake* and salt to a boil. Add flaked crab meat to warm up. Squeeze lightly.

3 Toss hot cooked rice with crab meat to mix evenly. Place this in each serving bowl and top with *kani-no-ko*. Scatter *shiso* seeds.

Hint: *Shiso* seeds can be substituted with *sanshou*(Japanese pepper) seeds.

CRAB *OYAKO* DONBURI *(Kani Oyako-don)*

CODFISH *OYAKO* DONBURI *(Tara Oyako-don)*

3-4 cups hot cooked rice (see p.6)
1 medium *tarako* (salted cod roe)
¼ filet *hidara* (dried codfish)
5-6 *shiso* leaves, shredded

Serves: 2

1 In a non-stick frying pan, cook *tarako* over low heat. When heated through, remove skin and crumble eggs.

2 Grill *hidara* on both sides briefly until soft and tear into fine strips.

3 Mix hot cooked rice with crumbled *tarako* eggs. Add shredded *shiso* and toss lightly. Place in each serving bowl and top with *hidara* strips.

Hint: Do not skin *tarako* before cooking. Eggs will splash when heated.

DONBURI CLASSICS

CONTENTS

CHICKEN-AND-EGG DONBURI
p.21
FISHERMEN'S CLAM DONBURI
p.21
PORK CUTLET DONBURI p.22
FRIED PRAWN DONBURI p.22
PORK CUTLET DONBURI
WITH *MISO* SAUCE p.23
BEEF BOWL p.24
TEMPURA DONBURI p.25
TERIYAKI EEL DONBURI p.25
BEEF AND VEGETABLE DONBURI
p.26
CLAM AND EGG DONBURI p.27

Here are typical everyday one-bowl dishes that most Japanese feel familiar with. These time tested classics can be called old family recipes. Use a good quality rice and *dashi* stock. Instant *dashi* powder is available now for quick preparation.

3-4 cups hot cooked rice (see p.6)
4 oz(120 g) chicken thigh
3 eggs, lightly stirred
½ onion, thinly sliced
COOKING BROTH
⎡ ⅔ cup *dashi* stock
⎢ 1 tsp sugar
⎢ 2½ Tbsp soy sauce
⎣ 2½ Tbsp *mirin*
2-3 stalks *mitsuba* (trefoil)

Serves: 2

1 Slice chicken into thin, bite-size pieces. Slice onion lengthwise. Cut *mitsuba* into 1"(2.5cm) lengths.

2 In a saucepan, bring COOKING BROTH ingredients to a boil. Add onion and chicken. Heat until cooked and spread evenly to fit the size of serving bowls. Swirl in beaten eggs. When eggs are partially set (do not stir during cooking), sprinkle with *mitsuba*. Immediately remove from heat, cover and let steam for 2 minutes.

3 In each serving bowl, place rice and topping.

CHICKEN-AND-EGG DONBURI *(Oyako-don)*
This popular meal is affectionately called "parent-and-child bowl" in Japanese.

FISHERMEN'S CLAM DONBURI *(Fukagawa-don)*

3-4 cups hot cooked rice (see p.6)
10 oz(300 g) shelled raw clams
1 knob ginger
1 Tbsp *sake*
50 ml soy sauce
1 Tbsp *mirin*
Scallions for garnish

Serves: 2

1 Shake clams in salted water to remove dirt and sand. Rinse in cold water; drain.

2 Peel ginger and shred finely. Slice scallions.

3 In a saucepan, bring *sake* and clams to a boil. Cook for a few minutes, and add soy sauce, *mirin*, and ginger shreds. Boil down until liquid is evaporated.

4 Mix clams in steaming rice, and toss well. Transfer into each serving bowl and garnish with scallions.

Fukagawa, Tokyo, was once known for its abundant shellfish, hence the name.

PORK CUTLET DONBURI
(*Katsu-don*)

3-4 cups hot cooked rice (see p.6)
2 thick (about ½", 1.5cm) slices pork tenderloin
   Salt and pepper
Coating (flour, egg, breadcrumbs)
Vegetable oil for deep-frying
1 small onion, thinly sliced
COOKING BROTH
⌈ ⅔ cups *dashi* stock
| 2½ Tbsp soy sauce
| ¾ Tbsp *mirin*
⌊ ½ Tbsp sugar
2 eggs, lightly beaten
Mitsuba (trefoil)

Serves: 2

1 Rub salt and pepper onto pork. Dust with flour, dip in egg, and coat with breadcrumbs. In hot oil, deep-fry until golden. Cut into bite-size pieces.

2 Bring COOKING BROTH ingredients to a boil; set aside.

3 In a small frying pan, lay onion slices and place a pork cutlet. Pour in half amount of cooking broth from the edge of pan. Heat to a full boil, and swirl in egg. Do not stir. Sprinkle with *mitsuba*, and place a lid. Cook about 30 seconds.

4 Place rice in each serving bowl, and cover with cutlet mixture, including the cooking sauce. Serve hot.

Hint: Make one portion at a time using a small pan, or two servings in a large pan and separate when serving.

3-4 cups hot cooked rice (see p.6)
4 deep-fried prawns
COOKING BROTH
⌈ ⅔ cups *dashi* stock
| 1 tsp sugar
⌊ 2½ Tbsp soy sauce
2½ Tbsp *mirin*
2 eggs, lightly beaten
Mitsuba (trefoil)

Serves: 2

1 In a small frying pan, heat COOKING BROTH ingredients to a boil. Lay deep-fried prawns and cook just until heated through (See above for deep-frying).

2 Swirl in beaten egg, sprinkle *mitsuba*, and cover; cook until the egg is half set. Place hot cooked rice in each serving bowl, and transfer prawn topping onto it.

FRIED PRAWN DONBURI
(*Ebi Fry Donburi*)
Try this style of dish with any fried food.

PORK CUTLET DONBURI WITH *MISO* SAUCE *(Miso-katsu-don)*

3-4 cups hot cooked rice (see p.6)
2 thick(about ½", 1.5cm) slices pork loin
   Salt and pepper
¼ long onion
Coating (flour, egg, breadcrumbs)
Vegetable oil fpr deep-frying
MISO SAUCE
⌈ ⅓ cup *dashi* stock
| 2 Tbsp *sake*
| 4 Tbsp *Haccho miso*
| 4 Tbsp sugar
| ½ Tbsp *mirin*
⌊ 1 Tbsp soy sauce   Serves: 2

1 In a saucepan, cook and stir *MISO* SAUCE ingredients over medium heat, until thickened.

2 Sprinkle pork with salt and pepper, dust with flour, coat with beaten egg, then with breadcrumbs. Deep-fry until golden brown.

3 Cut long onions into 2"(5 cm) lengths, shred lengthwise, and soak in cold water until crisp.

4 Place hot cooked rice in each serving bowl and lay sliced cutlet. Pour over Miso Sauce and garnish with drained onion.

Katsu-don

"Katsu" is a word adapted from the Western 'cutlet', deep-fried breaded meat. *"Katsu"* in Japanese literally means "to win", and is popular among youngsters, especially sport players. In 1921, at a Tokyo restaurant, a Waseda High School student hurriedly put a pork cutlet on rice and poured Worcestershire sauce over it. This is said to be the origin of this popular dish. Here is an interesting version with a sweet *miso* sauce from Nagoya, Aichi Prefecture.

BEEF BOWL (*Gyu-don*)

3-4 cups hot cooked rice (see p.6)
4 oz (120 g) loin beef, thinly sliced
½ package (3½ oz, 100 g) yam noodles *(shirataki)*
½ onion
COOKING BROTH
⎡½ cup *dashi* stock
⎜½ cup *mirin*
⎜1-2 Tbsp sugar
⎣½ cup soy sauce
Pickled ginger *(beni shoga)*

Serves: 2

1 Cut yam noodles into bite size lengths. Cook in boiling water 2 minutes to remove harshness; drain.

2 Cut peeled onion in half lengthwise, then into about ⅛"(3 mm) slices.

3 In a saucepan, bring COOKING BROTH ingredients to a boil. Add beef slices and cook, occasionally skimming scum.

3

4 Add yam noodles and cook for a few minutes. Add onion and cook a further 5 minutes. Place hot cooked rice in each serving bowl, and place topping and broth. Garnish with pickled ginger.

This simple dish has become Japan's top-selling *donburi*. Here is the original version.

TEMPURA DONBURI
(Ten-don)

3-4 cups hot cooked rice (see p.6)
4 large prawns, deveined
TEMPURA BATTER
⌈1 egg yolk
|1 cup ice-cold water
⌊1 heap cup all-purpose flour
Vegetable oil for deep-frying
SAUCE
⌈1⅔ cups *dashi* stock
|200 ml soy sauce
|100 ml *mirin*
⌊2 oz (60 g) sugar
Small peppers, optional

Serves: 2

Hint: Prepare rice and sauce before deep-frying so that you can enjoy the crispness of *tempura*.

This special treat is made simply with *tempura* dipped in delicate sauce.

1 Shell prawns, leaving the tails intact. To keep from curling, hold each prawn with both of your hands, and curl the other way than the natural curl, until the flesh is torn at two points.

2 Make *TEMPURA* BATTER. Stir egg yolk and water, then blend sifted flour only lightly.

3 Holding the tail end, dip the prawns in batter, then deep-fry in 350°F(180°C) oil until golden.

4 Bring SAUCE ingredients to a boil. Place hot cooked rice in each serving bowl, dip *tempura* in the sauce and immediately lay on the rice. Garnish with fried vegetable such as pepper.

4

TERIYAKI EEL DONBURI (Una-don)

3-4 hot cooked rice (see p.6)
4-5 oz (120-140 g) broiled eel (*unagi*)
2 Tbsp *sake* or water
Kabayaki-no-tare (sauce for broiled eels)
Sansho (Japanese pepper)
3-4 stalks chives or scallion
2 *kinome* (*sansho* sprout), optional

Serves: 2

1 Slice chives and set aside. In a heated frying pan, warm broiled eel with *sake* or water over low heat, covered. When liquid is evaporated, remove eel and cut into bite-size pieces.

2 Place hot cooked rice in each serving bowl, swirl in some sauce and arrange eel pieces. Pour sauce again, and garnish with chives and *kinome*.

Hint: Steaming process turns the eel tender and fluffy.

One of the most popular *donburi* made easy with prepared eel.

25

BEEF AND VEGETABLE DONBURI *(Gyu Yanagawa Donburi)*

3-4 cups hot cooked rice (see p.6)
½ lb (230 g) thinly sliced beef
½ *gobo* (burdock root)
4 *shiitake* mushrooms
2 eggs, lightly beaten
COOKING BROTH
⌈ ¾ cup *dashi* stock
⎪ 3 Tbsp light soy sauce
⎪ 3 Tbsp *sake*
⎣ 4 Tbsp *mirin*

Serves: 2

1 Cut sliced beef into ⅜" (1 cm) wide strips. Slice *shiitake* thinly as shown right. Shave burdock root and soak in water to remove harshness.

2 In a shallow saucepan or frying pan, heat COOKING BROTH ingredients to a boil. Add burdock and cook until tender. Add *shiitake* and beef and cook for 3 minutes.

3 Swirl in beaten eggs and continue to cook until half set. Do not stir. Serve hot on steaming rice.

This is a *donburi* version of traditional *Yanagawa-nabe*, a winter delicacy of old Tokyo.

CLAM AND EGG DONBURI *(Fukagawa-don Tamago-toji)*

1 Place clams in a colander and shake in salted water to remove dirt and sand. Rinse in cold water; drain.

2 To shave *gobo*, make slits lengthwise as shown below, and shave as if shaving a pencil, dropping into vinegared water.

3 Heat oil in a frying pan, add drained *gobo* shavings briefly. Add COOKING BROTH and cook for 5-6 minutes. Add clams and when they are swollen, swirl in beaten eggs (do not stir). Sprinkle with spring onion and *mitsuba*. Cover and remove from heat; let steam.

4 Place rice in each serving bowl, and cover it with clam topping and broth. Serve with 7-spice powder or cayenne pepper, if preferred.

Fukagawa Donburi
Edokko, or native downtown Tokyo-ites, had a reputation for being impatient, and this quick meal was their favorite when Fukagawa still faced the sea, long time ago.

3-4 cups hot cooked rice(see p.6)
5 oz (150 g) shelled raw clams
½ *gobo* (burdock root)
3-4 stalks spring onion, cut up
2 eggs, lightly beaten
Mitsuba (trefoil) or coriander
1 tsp vegetable oil
COOKING BROTH
⌈½ cup *dashi* stock
│1 Tbsp *sake*
│1 Tbsp *mirin*
│1 tsp sugar
│1 Tbsp soy sauce
⌊Pinch salt
Vinegar
7-spice powder or cayenne pepper

Serves: 2

LIGHT AND HEALTHY DONBURI

CONTENTS

CRISP BACON DONBURI p.29
SCALLION DONBURI p.29
BABY SARDINE DONBURI p.30
WILD PLANTS DONBURI p.30
SOBORO DONBURI p.31
MUSHROOM AND OKRA
                DONBURI p.32
MOLOHAIRE DONBURI p.32
NAMEKO DONBURI p.32
CHICKEN SALAD DONBURI p.33
ABURA-AGE DONBURI p34
SCRAMBLED EGG DONBURI p.35
YAKITORI DONBURI p.35

Time-saving one-bowl dishes introduced here use various canned or pouch-packed foods and are ideal for lunch or snacks as they are so easy to prepare, and of course, easy to clean up afterwards.

CRISP BACON DONBURI

3-4 cups hot cooked rice (see p.6)
3 strips bacon
1⅓ oz (40 g) *daikon* or other greens
Salt and pepper to taste
1 Tbsp vegetable oil

Serves: 2

1 Use any fresh or lightly pickled greens. If using *daikon* or other fresh greens, remove core, boil briefly in salted water, and blanch in cold water. Squeeze out water and cut up.

2 Heat oil in a frying pan, and cook cut-up bacon until crisp. Pat with paper towel as shown to remove excess grease.

3 Using the rendered grease of bacon, stir-fry greens and sprinkle with salt and pepper.

4 Place rice in each serving bowl, cover with greens, and place bacon on top.

Hint: This can be served hot or cold. Be sure to check the taste since saltiness is the key.

SCALLION DONBURI

3-4 cups cooked rice(see p.6)
2-3 stalks scallion
1 pouch (⅛-⅙ oz, 4-5g) *kezuribushi*
         (dried bonito shavings)
1 Tbsp vegetable oil
Salt and pepper
1 Tbsp soy sauce
Pickled ginger *(beni-shoga)*

Serves: 2

1 Heat oil in a frying pan, and stir-fry chopped scallion over low heat until the aroma is released.

2 Add cooked rice and stir-fry, separating the grains. Sprinkle with salt and pepper. Drizzle in soy sauce from the edges of the pan.

3 Transfer into each serving bowl and top with *kezuribushi* and pickled ginger.

Hint: To obtain the best flavor, do not overcook scallion.

BABY SARDINE DONBURI

3-4 cups cooked rice (see p.6)
1⅔ oz(50 g) *chirimenjako*
    (salted baby sardine)
3-4 stalks chives or scallion, sliced
½ Tbsp vegetable oil
1 tsp soy sauce
Kinome (*sansho* sprout), optional

Serves: 2

1 Heat oil in a frying pan, and stir-fry baby sardine over low heat until crisp. Drizzle in soy sauce from the edges of the pan.

2 In a bowl, put fried sardine, sliced chives and rice. Toss lightly and transfer into each serving bowl. Garnish with *kinome*, if preferred.

Hint: Crisp baby sardine makes a contrast with fluffy rice.

WILD PLANTS DONBURI *(Sansai Gohan)*

1½ cups uncooked rice
1 package (½ lb,230g) boiled *sansai*
    (mixed wild plants)
½ *abura-age* (thin fried *tofu*)
1 cup *dashi* stock
1½ Tbsp each, *sake*, sugar, and *mirin*
2 Tbsp soy sauce

Serves: 2-3

1 Wash rice and set in rice cooker. While cooking rice, prepare ingredients. Drain *sansai*. Douse *abura-age* with boiling water to remove excess oil, and shred.

2 In a saucepan, cook *sansai* and *abura-age* with *dashi*, *sake*, sugar, *mirin* and soy sauce over high heat just until the liquid is absorbed.

3 When rice cooker signs the end of cooking (just before steaming procedure), add drained *sansai* mixture and replace the lid. Let steam for 10-15 minutes.

4 Toss well and transfer into each serving bowl.

SOBORO DONBURI

3-4 cups hot cooked rice (see p.6)
½ lb (230 g) ground beef
SEASONING for beef
⎡2 Tbsp *dashi* stock
⎢1½ Tbsp *sake*
⎢2 Tbsp soy sauce
⎣1 Tbsp sugar
2 eggs, beaten
⎡1 Tbsp sugar
⎣Pinch salt
Frozen green peas

Serves: 2

Hint: Make a stripe, pinwheel, or whatever pattern for fun.

1 In a saucepan, cook ground beef with SEASONING ingredients, constantly stirring to crumble. Cook until the moisture is nearly gone.

2 Combine beaten eggs, sugar and salt, and scramble vigorously, using 2 pairs of chopsticks as shown.

3 Pour green peas with boiling water to thaw.

4 Place hot cooked rice in each serving bowl, and cover with beef and egg, pressing slightly. Decorate with green peas or pickled ginger.

2

MUSHROOM AND OKRA DONBURI
(Nametake Donburi)

3-4 cups hot cooked rice (see p.6)
1⅔ oz(50 g) *nametake*, jarred
4 pods okra
Pinch salt
Nori seaweed, shredded

Serves: 2

Note: *Nametake* is a jarred type *enokidake* mushrooms, usually seasoned with soy sauce and *mirin*. It goes with well plain rice or grated *daikon* radish.

1 Rub okra with salt to remove the surface "hair". Douse with boiling water and slice thinly.

2 In a bowl, toss hot rice with *nametake* and okra. Check the taste and sprinkle with salt, if needed. Transfer into each serving bowl and sprinkle with shredded *nori* seaweed.

MOLOHAIRE DONBURI

3-4 cups hot cooked rice (see p.6)
1 package molohaire greens
   Pinch salt
1 package *natto* (fermented soybeans)
⌈ ⅔ Tbsp soy sauce
⌊ ½ tsp hot mustard paste
Kezuribushi (dried bonito shavings)

Serves: 2

Hint: Use only leaves of molohaire.

1 Rinse molohaire thoroughly and snip off leaves. Discard stems. Blanch in boiling water with the salt and drain in a colander.

2 Mix *natto* with soy sauce and mustard, stirring well. In a bowl, combine molohaire and *natto* lightly.

3 Place hot rice in each serving bowl, and mound the molohaire and *natto* mixture. Top with *kezuribushi*.

NAMEKO DONBURI
(Nameko Oroshi-ae Donburi)

3-4 cups hot cooked rice (see p.6)
1 package *nameko* mushrooms
¼ *daikon* radish
Yuzu citron as garnish

Serves: 2

Hint: Drain grated *daikon* radish well.

1 Place *nameko* mushrooms in a colander, and douse with boiling water. This removes excess sliminess.

MOLOHAIRE DONBURI

NAMEKO DONBURI

CHICKEN SALAD DONBURI

CHICKEN SALAD DONBURI

2 Grate *daikon* radish and combine with mushrooms. Place over hot cooked rice and garnish with shredded *yuzu* citron. Serve with soy sauce.

3-4 cups hot cooked rice (see p.6)
4 oz (120 g) chicken fillets
⌈Lemon juice
⎢1 tsp *sake*
⌊Pinch salt
½ cucumber
DRESSING
⌈2 Tbsp mayonnaise
⎢1 tsp soy sauce
⎢⅓ tsp hot mustard paste
⌊1 tsp *sake*

Serves: 2

1 Cook chicken in boiling water, skimming occasionally. Drain and tear into fine strips. Sprinkle with lemon juice, *sake* and salt.

2 Slice cucumber very thinly at a slant. Shred the stack of slices to make evenly skinned, fine strips.

3 Blend DRESSING ingredients in a small bowl.

4 Place hot cooked rice in each serving bowl, and arrange cucumber strips. Arrange chicken strips on top and pour over the dressing.

33

ABURA-AGE DONBURI *(Kitsune Donburi)*

3-4 cups hot cooked rice (see p.6)
1 *abura-age* (thin fried *tofu*)
  2 Tbsp soy sauce
4 *shiitake* mushrooms
COOKING BROTH for *shiitake*
⌈100 ml *dashi* stock
|1½ Tbsp soy sauce
⌊1 Tbsp sugar
4 *shiso* leaves, shredded
Small knob of ginger, grated

Serves: 2

Note: Deep-fried, thinly sliced *tofu* was supposed to be a favorite of fox, or *kitsune*, hence the name.

1 Discard stems of *shiitake* mushrooms. Combine COOKING BROTH ingredients and cook *shiitake* until the liquid is almost gone. Slice and keep warm.

2 Grill *abura-age* over low flame, or broil in toaster oven, until the surface is crisp. Turn over and grill the other side. Dip in soy sauce to coat all over. Cut in half lengthwise, then slice into ⅜"(1 cm) widths.

3 Place hot cooked rice in each serving bowl and arrange *shiitake* and *abura-age* slices. Garnish with shredded *shiso* leaves and grated ginger.

Hint: Dip *abura-age* in soy sauce just after grilling.

SCRAMBLED EGG DONBURI

3-4 cups hot cooked rice (see p.6)
4 oz (120 g) young pea greens or spinach
2 eggs, beaten
   Salt and pepper
1 Tbsp vegetable oil
DRESSING
  2 Tbsp soy sauce
  ½ Tbsp rice vinegar
  Pinch sugar
  ¼ tsp hot mustard paste
  ½ tsp sesame oil

Serves: 2

1 Cook greens briefly in salted boiling water, then plunge into cold water and squeeze out water; cut up.

2 Heat vegetable oil in a frying pan. Add salt and pepper to beaten eggs, and scramble in the pan. Mix with cut-up greens.

3 Combine DRESSING ingredients and add to scrambled egg mixture as shown. Transfer onto hot cooked rice and serve.

YAKITORI DONBURI

3-4 cups hot cooked rice (see p.6)
5 oz (140 g) canned or packaged *yakitori*
          (grilled chicken on skewers)
¼ long onion
6-8 small peppers
Vegetable oil
7-spice powder, optional

Serves: 2

1 Warm *yakitori* in microwave oven or grill.

2 Cut long onion into 1¼-1½" (3.5-4cm) lengths. Heat oil in a frying pan and add long onion and peppers. Cook until browned.

3 Place hot cooked rice in each serving bowl, and arrange *yakitori*, long onion and peppers over it. Sprinkle with 7-spice powder, if preferred.

Hint: Before warming *yakitori*, sprinkle them with *sake* to enhance the flavor.

35

NOURISHING DONBURI

CONTENTS

FRIED SCALLOP DONBURI p.37
CHICKEN *TERIYAKI* DONBURI
                      p.37
TARAMO DONBURI p.38
MAPO DONBURI p.38
SUKIYAKI DONBURI p.39
ATSU-AGE DONBURI p.40
SWEET SOUR SHRIMP DONBURI
                      p.41
FRIED CHICKEN DONBURI p.41
STIR-FRIED CHICKEN AND
   MUSHROOM DONBURI p.42
CHEESY SQUID DONBURI p.43
MIXED *TEMPURA* DONBURI p.43
CURRIED *TOFU* DONBURI p.44
GINGER OYSTER DONBURI p.45

Here you will find rich and tasty rice-bowl-meals that will satisfy the stomachs of hard workers or growing youths. Most of the meat or fish toppings are combined with nutritious vegetables including *tofu* and mushrooms. Adjust the volume of veggies depending on the person's appetite.

FRIED SCALLOP DONBURI

3-4 cups hot cooked rice (see p.6)
6 large scallops
    Salt and pepper
¼ onion, sliced
Mitsuba (trefoil), cut up
2 eggs, beaten
Coating (flour, egg, breadcrumbs)
Vegetable oil for deep-frying
COOKING BROTH
⌈¾ cup *dashi* stock
│1½ Tbsp soy sauce
│½ Tbsp sugar
⌊1 Tbsp *mirin*

Serves: 2

1 Cut scallops into half thicknesses. Sprinkle with salt and pepper. Dust each piece with flour, dip in beaten egg, and coat with breadcrumbs.

2 Heat oil to 350°F(180°C) and deep-fry scallops until crisp and golden.

3 In a frying pan, bring COOKING BROTH ingredients to a boil, add sliced

onion, and cook for 2 minutes. Add deep-fried scallops and immediately swirl in beaten eggs. Sprinkle with *mitsuba* and cook until egg is partially cooked but still runny.

4 Transfer gently onto hot cooked rice mounded in each serving bowl.

Hint: Do not stir egg in the pan and leave it soft and juicy.

CHICKEN *TERIYAKI* DONBURI

3-4 cups hot cooked rice (see p.6)
½lb (230 g) chicken breast
MARINADE
⌈1 Tbsp *sake*
│1 Tbsp soy sauce
⌊½ Tbsp ginger juice
1 Tbsp vegetable oil
TERIYAKI SAUCE
⌈1 Tbsp *mirin*
│1 Tbsp sugar
⌊2 Tbsp soy sauce
Sesame seeds, toasted

Serves: 2

Hint: Prick the skin of chicken so the sauce will be absorbed well.

1 Using a fork, prick over the skin side of chicken. Coat with MARINADE and let stand for 30 minutes, turning once.

2 Heat vegetable oil in a frying pan, and sauté drained chicken until lightly browned. Reduce heat, add *TERIYAKI* SAUCE and cook about 7 minutes over medium heat, covered.

3 When the chicken is cooked, remove the lid and cook over high heat to thicken the sauce. Slice chicken.

4 Place hot cooked rice in each serving bowl, and drizzle in remaining *teriyaki* sauce from the pan. Arrange chicken slices on top and sprinkle with sesame seeds.

37

TARAMO DONBURI

3-4 cups hot cooked rice (see p.6)
5 oz(150 g) potatoes
1 Tbsp green peas, frozen or canned
1 lightly salted cod roe (*tarako*)
1 cup water
1 Tbsp sugar
1 Tbsp soy sauce

Serves: 2

1 Cut potatoes into bite-size pieces. Soak in water.

2 Make a lengthwise slit into the cod roe, and slice as shown, so the inside will be crumbled easily.

3 In a saucepan, bring the water to a boil with sugar, add drained potato pieces until tender.

4 Add cod roe, crumbling with a fork. Mix with potato evenly. Add soy sauce and cook until the moisture is almost gone. Transfer onto hot cooked rice.

Hint: Adjust the amount of soy sauce depending on the saltiness of cod roe.

MAPO DONBURI

3-4 cups hot cooked rice (see p.6)
½ cake *tofu* (firm type)
2 oz(60 g) ground beef
3-4 stalks *nira* (garlic chives)
COOKING SAUCE
⌈1 tsp tienmen jang (sweet bean paste)
│¼ tsp toban jang (hot bean paste)
│1 Tbsp soy sauce
⌊⅓ cup chicken stock
1 Tbsp vegetable oil
½ tsp cornstarch, dissolved in ½ Tbsp water

Serves: 2

Hint: Adjust the spiciness with toban jang.

1 Slice *tofu* into half thicknesses, then into ¾"(2 cm) cubes. Drain well in a colander.

2 In a small bowl, combine COOKING SAUCE ingredients for quick cooking. Chop garlic chives.

3 Heat vegetable oil in a wok or frying pan, sauté ground beef. Add cooking sauce and bring to a gentle

boil. Add *tofu* and cook about 5 minutes over medium heat.

4 Stir in dissolved cornstarch and garlic chives. Mix lightly and remove from heat. Transfer gently onto hot cooked rice.

SUKIYAKI DONBURI

3-4 cups hot cooked rice (see p.6)
5 oz(150 g) beef sirloin, sliced paper-thin
½ package (3⅓ oz, 100g)yam noodles
(*shirataki*)
¼ bunch edible chrysanthemum leaves
½ long onion
2 *shiitake* mushrooms, stems removed
½ cake grilled *tofu*
2 Chinese cabbage leaves
1 Tbsp vegetable oil
100 ml *Sukiyaki* Sauce (commercial)

Serves: 2

Note: *Sukiyaki* sauce can be made easily at home: Combine 1 cup *dashi* stock, ¼ cup each *mirin* and soy sauce, and 1½ Tbsp sugar. Bring to a boil and cook until slightly thickened, for about 3 minutes.

1 Cut beef into bite-size pieces. Also cut chrysanthemum leaves likewise, as shown.

2 Parboil yam noodles about 2 minutes. Make a criss-cross incision into the caps of *shiitake* mushrooms. Slice long onions diagonally into 1"(2.5 cm) thicknesses. Cut up Chinese cabbage. Slice grilled *tofu*.

3 Heat vegetable oil in a saucepan, and briefly saute beef, long onion, yam noodles, Chinese cabbage and chrysanthemum leaves in order. Immediately pour in *Sukiyaki* Sauce and add grilled *tofu*. Simmer until the sauce is absorbed well.

4 Place hot cooked rice in each serving bowl, and arrange *sukiyaki* on top and pour in remaining sauce, if any.

Sukiyaki

Sukiyaki has a short history, since meat was forbidden in old times. Some people secretly enjoyed eating game meats outdoors using thieir hoes (*suki*) as a cooking pan. Since a visiting American statesman had a cow slaughtered for the first time for food in the late nineteenth century, this one-pot dish suddenly became popular, and there are quite a few restaurants that specialize in *sukiyaki*. When cooking, each ingredient is kept separate and not stirred. Adjust the taste by adding soy sauce, *sake* or sugar to your liking.

ATSU-AGE DONBURI

3-4 cups hot cooked rice (see p.6)
1 *atsu-age* (thick fried *tofu*, about 10 oz/
  300 g)
⌈2 cups *dashi* stock
 2 tsp sugar
 ½ Tbsp *mirin*
⌊1 Tbsp soy *sauce*
4-5 green beans, strung
2 *shiitake* mushrooms, stems removed
2 oz(60 g) ground chicken
⌈1 tsp ginger juice
 1 Tbsp *sake*
 ½ Tbsp sugar
⌊1 Tbsp soy sauce
2 tsp cornstarch, dissolved in 1 Tbsp
  water

Serves: 2

Hint: Simmer fried *tofu* slowly as it does
not absorb the sauce immediately, and
also it may stick to the bottom of pan if
cooked over high heat.

1 Douse fried *tofu* with boiling water to remove excess oil. Cut lengthwise in half and then into ⅜"(1 cm) slices.

2 In a saucepan, heat *dashi* stock, sugar, *mirin* and soy sauce to a boil, and add fried *tofu* slices. Simmer until the broth is almost gone.

3 Cut *shiitake* into 2"(5 cm) squares. Parboil greeen beans in salted water briefly, and cut diagonally into thin slices.

4 In a saucepan, heat *dashi* stock and ground chicken. Crumble and bring to a boil. Skim the surface. Add *shiitake* and cook about 2 minutes. Add ginger juice, *sake*, sugar and soy sauce. Simmer a further 2 minutes

and stir in dissolved cornstarch. Stir quickly so the sauce is evenly thickened.

5 Place hot cooked rice in each serving bowl, and arrange fried *tofu* slices over it. Pour chicken sauce over and sprinkle with sliced green beans.

SWEET SOUR SHRIMP DONBURI

Hint: For dusting, use as little cornstarch as possible since the thick sauce contains cornstarch as well.

3-4 cups hot cooked rice (see p.6)
1 Tbsp dried black fungus
1 Tbsp green peas, canned or frozen
2 Tbsp vegetable oil
5 oz(150 g) shelled shrimp
⌈Pinch salt
⌊½ egg white, beaten
1 Tbsp cornstarch for dusting
COOKING SAUCE
⌈1 tsp soy sauce
│1½ Tbsp each rice vinegar and sugar
│¼ tsp salt
⌊Pinch chicken bouillon granules
1 tsp cornstarch, dissolved in 2 tsp water
Vegetable oil for deep-frying   Serves: 2

1 Rinse shrimp in water. Devein and drain. Combine egg white and salt, and marinate shrimp about 10 minutes.

2 Soak fungus in hot water until softened.

3 Dust shrimp with cornstarch, and deep-fry in 340°F(°C) oil until crisp, dropping a few at a time.

4 Heat 2 Tbsp vegetable oil in a frying pan, and sauté drained fungus. Add COOKING SAUCE ingredients and bring to a boil. Stir in dissolved cornstarch to thicken the sauce. Add drained peas and shrimp, and stir quickly.

5 Place hot cooked rice in each serving bowl, and arrange the topping.

FRIED CHICKEN DONBURI

3-4 cups hot cooked rice (see p.6)
5 oz(150 g) chicken thigh
⌈1 Tbsp *sake*
⌊1 Tbsp soy sauce
Cornstarch for dusting
Vegetable oil for deep-frying
Lettuce leaves
2"(5 cm) *daikon* radish
Lemon wedges

Serves: 2

Hint: Grated *daikon* mixed with fried chicken lessens the greasiness.

1 Cut chicken into bite-size pieces. Marinate in *sake* and soy sauce for 20-30 minutes.

2 Tear lettuce leaves, soak in ice water until crisp; drain. Peel and grate *daikon* radish and drain.

3 Drain chicken and dust with cornstarch. Deep-fry in 340°F(170°C) oil until golden ; drain oil.

4 Place hot cooked rice in each serving bowl, lay lettuce leaves, and arrange fried chicken. Top with grated *daikon* radish. Serve with lemon wedges and soy sauce.

STIR-FRIED CHICKEN AND MUSHROOM DONBURI

3-4 cups hot cooked rice (see p.6)
7 oz(200 g) chicken breast
½ bunch bok choy
1 package *shimeji* mushrooms
COOKING BROTH
⌈ ½ cup chicken stock
| 1 Tbsp *sake*
⌊ 2 Tbsp soy sauce
1 tsp cornstarch, dissolved in 1 Tbsp water
1 Tbsp sesame oil
1 Tbsp vegetable oil

Serves: 2

1 Divide bok choy into stalks and leaves. Slice stalks lengthwise.

2 Remove base of *shimeji* mushrooms and break into pieces.

3 Cut chicken into small, bite-size pieces. Heat vegetable oil in a frying pan, and sauté chicken. When chicken turns white, add bok choy stalks and *shimeji* and stir-fry.

4 When chicken is cooked, stir in bok choy leaves. Add COOKING BROTH ingredients and bring to a boil. Stir in dissolved cornstarch, and sprinkle in sesame oil. Remove from heat.

5 Place hot cooked rice in each serving bowl, and place the topping.

Hint: Sauté bok choy lastly to keep the fresh green color.

CHEESY SQUID DONBURI

3-4 cups hot cooked rice (see p.6)
1 squid, tentacles removed (about 4 oz/ 120 g)
2 bell peppers
½ onion
1 Tbsp vegetable oil
Salt and pepper
½ cup tomato ketchup
2"(60 g) natural cheese, shredded
Parsley, minced

Serves: 2

1 Skin squid and slice into ⅜"(1 cm) rings.

2 Remove top and seeds of bell peppers, and cut lengthwise into 8. Slice onion thinly.

3 Heat vegetable oil in a frying pan, sauté pepper and onion slices only briefly. Add squid and cook. Sprinkle with salt and pepper.

4 Add ketchup and stir-fry. Finally, stir in shredded cheese. When cheese melts and threads, remove from heat.

5 Serve over hot cooked rice, garnished with minced parsley.

MIXED *TEMPURA* DONBURI

3-4 cups hot cooked rice (see p.6)
½ medium onion
4 oz(120 g) shelled shrimp
Chrysanthemum leaves, optional
Shiso(perilla) leaves, optional
TEMPURA BATTER
⎡½ beaten egg plus ice water
⎢   to measure 100 ml
⎣½ cup all-purpose flour
Vegetable oil for deep-frying
SAUCE
⎡¼ cup *mirin*
⎢2 Tbsp soy sauce
⎣½ Tbsp sugar

Serves: 2

1 In a saucepan, bring SAUCE ingredients to a boil; set aside.

2 Slice onion thinly. Devein shrimp, if any, and drain.

3 Make *TEMPURA* BATTER. In a bowl, combine egg and ice water well. Add flour and mix lightly.

4 Heat oil to 325° F(160° C). Dip only one side of chrysanthemum leaf in batter, and slide into oil, battered side down. Deep-fry until crisp, turning once. Deep-fry *shiso* leaves in the same manner.

5 Add onion and shrimp to the batter, and mix to coat evenly. Using a large spoon, drop a quarter portion into hot oil, and deep-fry until crisp.

6 Place hot cooked rice in each serving bowl. Lay mixed *tempura* on rice, and pour over warmed sauce.

Hint: The vivid green color of *shiso*, chrysanthemum leaves, or peppers is not spoiled if deep-fried in lower temperature oil (around 325° F/160° C).

CURRIED *TOFU* DONBURI

3-4 cups hot cooked rice (see p.6)
½ cake *tofu* (firm type)
3 oz(90 g) shelled shrimp, deveined
Cornstarch for dusting
½ package *shimeji* mushrooms
¼ onion
1 bell pepper
COOKING SAUCE
⌈1 cup *dashi* stock
⎮3 Tbsp or less *mirin*
⎮3 Tbsp or less soy sauce
⌊Curry powder
1 tsp cornstarch, dissolved in 2 tsp
  water

Serves: 2

1 Cut *tofu* into small cubes. Boil in salted water, and take out when floating to the surface as shown.

2 Separate *shimeji* mushrooms. Seed and slice bell pepper into thin rounds. Slice onion thinly.

3 Dust shrimp in cornstarch and boil briefly.

4 In a saucepan, bring COOKING SAUCE ingredients to a boil. Add vegetables and shrimp. Add curry powder, adjusting to your taste.

5 Add *tofu* and cook briefly. Stir in dissolved cornstarch.

6 Place hot cooked rice in each serving bowl, and cover with the *tofu* mixture.

Hint: *Tofu* does not break easily if parboiled briefly.

GINGER OYSTER DONBURI

3-4 cups hot cooked rice (see p.6)
5 oz(150 g) shucked oysters
1 bok choy
1 knob ginger
2 Tbsp *sake*
1 Tbsp vegetable oil
COOKING SAUCE
⌈1½ Tbsp soy sauce
│2 Tbsp *sake*
│1 Tbsp oyster sauce
⌊1 Tbsp sugar
2 tsp cornstarch, dissolved in 1 Tbsp water
1 tsp vegetable oil
Salt and pepper

Serves: 2

1 Place oysters in a colander, and shake in sated water; rinse briefly in water and drain. Peel ginger knob and cut into halves. Slice one half for cooking, and shred the other half for garnish. Cut up bok choy and boil briefly in salted water; drain.

2 In a small saucepan, put oysters and *sake*. Cover and cook about 3 minutes.

3 Heat 1 Tbsp oil in a frying pan, and fry ginger slices and oysters with the juice. Add COOKING SAUCE ingredients and bring to a boil. Remove oysters and set aside.

4 Simmer the sauce until thickened, then put back oysters to absorb the flavor. Stir in dissolved cornstarch.

5 Heat 1 tsp oil in another frying pan, and stir-fry bok choy. Sprinkle with salt and pepper. Place over hot cooked rice, and top with oysters. Garnish with shredded ginger.

45

POWER DONBURI

CONTENTS
PORK AND CABBAGE DONBURI
p.47
PORK AND KIMCHEE DONBURI
p.47
BEEF AND ASPARAGUS
DONBURI p.48
SQUID DONBURI p.48
GARLIC STEAK DONBURI p.49
PORK *MISO* DONBURI p.49
GINGER PORK DONBURI p.50
BEEF AND ONION DONBURI
p.50
GARLIC OMELET DONBURI p.51
MAYONNAISE PORK DONBURI
p.51

Delicious, stamina-builing toppings are shown here with richly seasoned pork, beef, squid and egg. Whenever you feel tired or need an extra power, try these simple-to-make, easy-to-eat *donburi* dishes. A green vegetable is combined with most of them for health.

PORK AND CABBAGE DONBURI

3-4 cups hot cooked rice (see p.6)
4 oz(120 g) thinly sliced pork
⌈Salt and pepper
⌊Cornstarch for dusting
3 large leaves cabbage
COOKING SAUCE
⌈½ tsp ginger juice
|1 Tbsp *sake*
|1 Tbsp soys sauce
⌊1 Tbsp *mirin*
1 Tbsp vegetable oil
7-spice powder, optional

Serves: 2

Hint: Do not overcook cabbage so as to leave it crisp and tender.

1 Cut sliced pork into bite-size pieces and sprinkle with salt and pepper. Dust with cornstarch.

2 Cut cabbage leaves into bite-size pieces and set aside.

3 Heat oil in a frying pan and sauté pork. When pork is cooked, add cabbage and stir-fry briefly. Add COOKING SAUCE ingredients and cook.

4 Place hot cooked rice in each serving bowl, and top with the cabbage and pork together with the remaining juice. Sprinkle with 7-spice powder, if preferred.

PORK AND KIMCHEE DONBURI

3-4 cups hot cooked rice (see p.6)
5 oz (150 g) thinly sliced pork
½ long onion, diagonally sliced
7 oz (200 g) Chinese cabbage kimchee
¼ tsp grated garlic
1 tsp sesame seeds, toasted
1 Tbsp sesame oil
¼ Tbsp sugar
1 Tbsp soy sauce
Dash pepper

Serves: 2

Hint: Adjust the seasonings depending on the taste of kimchee.

1 Cut kimchee (do not wash) into about 1"(2.5 cm) widths. Cut pork slices into bite-size pieces. Mix with grated garlic and sesame seeds.

2 Heat sesame oil in a frying pan, sauté pork slices. Add sliced onion and kimchee. Add sugar, soy sauce and pepper, and stir-fry so the flavor is absorbed. Transfer onto hot cooked rice mounded in each serving bowl.

BEEF AND ASPARAGUS DONBURI

3-4 cups hot cooked rice (see p.6)
5 oz (150 g) thinly sliced beef
[Salt and pepper
⌊1 tsp *sake*
1 bunch asparagus
4"(10 cm) long onion
1 small knob ginger, sliced
COOKING SAUCE
[½ Tbsp oyster sauce
1 Tbsp soy sauce
1 Tbsp *sake*
½ tsp sugar
⌊2 Tbsp chicken stock
1½ tsp cornstarch, dissolved in 1 Tbsp
   water
2 Tbsp vegetable oil for stir-frying

Serves: 2

1 Cut beef slices into bite-size pieces. Sprinkle with salt, pepper and sake. Coat with ¼ Tbsp vegetable oil; set aside.

2 Discard tough ends of asparagus, and slice diagonally. Slice long onion diagonally.

3 Heat 1 Tbsp oil in a frying pan, and stir-fry asparagus briefly and remove.

4 In a small bowl, combine COOKING SAUCE ingredients.

5 Heat 1 Tbsp oil in the frying pan; and fry long onion and ginger. Add beef and sauté. When the beef is cooked, Stir in combined cooking sauce. Add asparagus.

6 Place hot cooked rice in each serving bowl, and cover with the beef topping.

Hint: When buying asparagus, select ones with fresh cut ends.

---

1 Remove inside of squid and the skin. Cut open and make criss-cross scores diagonally all over the surface. Cut into bite-size pieces. Cut garlic shoots into about 1"(2.5 cm) lengths.

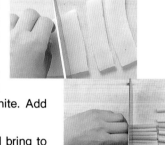

2 Heat sesame oil in a wok, and fry garlic until the aroma is released. Add squid and stir-fry until the color turns white. Add garlic shoots and stir-fry for a minute.

3 Add COOKING SAUCE ingredients and bring to a boil. Stir in dissolved cornstarch to thicken the sauce. Transfer onto hot cooked rice.

SQUID DONBURI

3-4 cups hot cooked rice (see p.6)
1 squid, tentacles removed
1 bunch garlic shoots
1 clove garlic, sliced
COOKING SAUCE
[1 Tbsp soy sauce
½ tsp chicken bouillon granules
¼ cup water
Salt and pepper
⌊Ginger juice
1 Tbsp sesame oil
½ tsp cornstarch, dissolved in 1 tsp water

Serves: 2

GARLIC STEAK DONBURI

3-4 cups cooked rice (see p.6)
2 beef rib or rib eye steaks
2 cloves garlic, sliced
Beef fat for sautéing
2 Tbsp red wine
2 Tbsp soy sauce
1 Tbsp butter
Salt and pepper
Watercress as garnish

Serves: 2

1 Rub steaks with salt and pepper. Heat beef fat in a frying pan, and sauté half of garlic slices until the aroma is released. Add beef steaks and sear both sides over high heat. Reduce heat and continue to cook until desired doneness. Pour off any fat in the pan. Add wine and soy sauce, then remove from heat.

2 Make garlic rice. Melt butter in a clean pan, and sauté remaining garlic slices. Add rice. Cook and stir over high heat, and season with salt and pepper.

3 Transfer garlic rice into each serving bowl, and top with sliced steak. Garnish with watercress sprigs.

Hint: Garlic rice enhances the flavor of this pan-broiled steak.

PORK *MISO* DONBURI

3-4 cups hot cooked rice (see p.6)
7 oz(200 g) thinly sliced pork
⌈ ½ Tbsp soy sauce
⌊ ½ tsp *mirin*
1-2 stalks chives or scallion
MISO SAUCE
⌈ ½ stalk long onion
│ 2 Tbsp *miso*
│ 1 Tbsp sugar
⌊ 1 Tbsp *sake*
1 Tbsp vegetable oil

Serves: 2

Hint: Use light-colored *miso*.

1 In a bowl, combine soy sauce and *mirin*. Mix in pork slices and set aside.

2 Slice long onion thinly and combine with *miso*, sugar and *sake*.

3 Heat oil in a frying pan, and drain and sauté pork slices. Add to *miso* sauce and toss well.

4 Place hot cooked rice in each serving bowl, and cover with dressed pork. Sprinkle with sliced chives.

49

GINGER PORK DONBURI

3-4 cups hot cooked rice (see p.6)
5 oz (150 g) thinly sliced pork loin
⌈ 2 Tbsp soy sauce
| 2 Tbsp *sake*
⌊ ½ tsp ginger juice
2 cabbage leaves
Vegetable oil for greasing

Serves: 2

Hint: Shredded cabbage makes a good contrast with the juicy pork.

1 Cut pork into bite-sized pieces. Marinate in soy sauce, *sake* and ginger juice (grate ginger and squeeze out) about 10 minutes. Shred cabbage leaves.

2 Heat vegetable oil in a frying pan. Sauté drained pork slices.

3 Place hot cooked rice in each serving bowl, and cover with shredded cabbage. Arrange pork on top.

4 In the frying pan, heat the marinade to a boil. Pour over pork.

BEEF AND ONION DONBURI

3-4 cups hot cooked rice (see p.6)
5 oz(150 g) thinly sliced beef
½ onion, thinly sliced
1/2 clove garlic, sliced
3 Tbsp tomato ketchup
½ Tbsp Worcester sauce
Salt and pepper
1 Tbsp butter
Parsley, minced

Serves: 2

1 Cut beef into 1-1⅛" (2.5-3 cm) wide strips.

2 Melt butter in a frying pan. Fry garlic slices until the aroma is released. Add sliced onion and fry until transparent. Add beef and stir-fry briefly.

3 Stir in ketchup, Worcester sauce, salt and pepper. Check the taste.

4 Place hot cooked rice in each serving bowl, and cover with beef topping. Sprinkle with minced parsley.

Hint: Fry onion until transparent, which enhances the overall flavor.

GARLIC OMELET DONBURI

3-4 cups hot cooked rice (see p.6)
2 oz(60 g) garlic chives
3 eggs
⎡1 Tbsp soy sauce
⎢2 Tbsp *dashi* stock
⎣2 tsp sugar
1 Tbsp vegetable oil

Serves: 2

1 Cut garlic chives into 1⅛"(3 cm) lengths. Beat eggs lightly.

2 Place hot cooked rice in each serving bowl. Cover and set aside.

3 Heat vegetable oil in a frying pan. Stir-fry garlic chives only for a few seconds and add *dashi* stock, soy sauce and sugar. Stir in beaten eggs and remove from heat immediately. Place on the rice and serve hot.

Hint: Do not overcook garlic chives as it becomes stringy.

MAYONNAISE PORK DONBURI

3-4 cups hot cooked rice (see p.6)
5 oz(150 g) thinly sliced pork
⎡2 tsp *sake*
⎣2 tsp soy sauce
1 bell pepper
1 Tbsp mayonnaise
Pinch salt
2 tsp vegetable oil

Serves: 2

1 Cut pork into bite-sized pieces. Marinate pork in *sake* and soy sauce for about 5 minutes.

2 Seed bell pepper and cut lengthwise into thin strips.

3 Heat oil in a frying pan. Fry pepper briefly and add pork slices. When pork is cooked, stir in mayonnaise and salt. Check the taste.

4 Place hot cooked rice in each serving bowl, and cover with pork mixture.

SPICY DONBURI

CONTENTS
STEWED OCTOPUS DONBURI
                        p.52
SICHUAN SHRIMP DONBURI
                        p.53
SPICY PORK-*SHABUSHABU*
              DONBURI p.53
SICHUAN PICKLE DONBURI p.54
SPICY GROUND MEAT DONBURI
                        p.54
CURRY DONBURI p.55
BIBIMBUP p.56
TOFU AND PORK DONBURI
                        p.56
SPICY CHICKEN DONBURI p.57
GARLIC OCTOPUS DONBURI
                        p.57
SPICY VERMICELLI DONBURI
                        p.57

A myriad of ethnic seasonings and spices are available today. This section introduces appetizing recipes utilizing the seasonings from various countries. Enjoy the marvelous combinations with plain steamed rice.

STEWED OCTOPUS DONBURI

3-4 cups hot cooked rice (see p.6)
½ lb (230 g) boiled octopus
½ onion, chopped
1 clove garlic, minced
1 small knob of ginger, minced
1 can (14 oz/400 g) tomatoes
Dash basil leaves, crushed
1 bay leaf
2 Tbsp white wine
1 Tbsp olive oil
2 bell peppers
Salt and pepper

Serves: 2

1 Cut octopus into large, bite-sized pieces. Cut peppers into 1"(2.5cm) squares.

2 Heat olive oil in a frying pan, and fry garlic and ginger. Add onion and fry until transparent.

3 Add octopus and sauté briefly. Sprinkle with wine. Add tomatoes, basil and bay leaf. Reduce heat and simmer for about 20 minutes.

4 Remove bay leaf. Add bell pepper. Adjust the taste with salt and pepper.

5 Place hot cooked rice in each serving bowl, and cover with stewed octopus.

Hint: Be sure to fry aromatic herbs first and cook onion slowly until transparent.

SICHUAN SHRIMP DONBURI

3-4 cups hot cooked rice (see P.6)
3½ oz(100 g) shelled shrimp
1 Tbsp frozen green peas
½ tsp minced garlic
½ tsp minced ginger
Salt and pepper
1 tsp vegetable oil
CHILI SAUCE
- 3 Tbsp tomato ketchup
- 1 tsp sugar
- ½ Tbsp soy sauce
- ½ Tbsp sesame oil
- ⅓ Tbsp toban jang (hot bean paste)
- 1 tsp chicken stock granules
- ½ cup water
2 tsp cornstarch, dissolved in 4 tsp water

Serves: 2

Hint: Use unsalted fresh shrimp. Frozen green peas show more vivid green than canned ones.

1 Rinse shrimp in salty water and drain; sprinkle with salt and pepper.

2 Heat vegetable oil in a frying pan until very hot, and fry garlic and ginger. Stir-fry shrimp and green peas.

3 Combine CHILI SAUCE ingredients in a small bowl, and add to the pan. Stir in dissolved cornstarch and cook until the sauce thickens.
4 Place hot cooked rice in each serving bowl, and top with shrimp and sauce.

SPICY PORK-*SHABUSHABU* DONBURI

3-4 cups hot cooked rice (see p.6)
5 oz(150 g) pork loin, cut paper thin
DRESSING
- 2 tsp kochu jang
- 1 tsp sesame oil
- 2 tsp soy sauce
2 ” (5cm) long onion
1 Tbsp toasted sesame seed
4 scallions, sliced

Serves: 2

1 Cook pork briefly in boiling water, and slice into strips. Combine DRESSING ingredients in a bowl and add the pork; set aside.

2 Cut long onion lengthwise into skin, and remove the core. Layer the skin and shred finely, as shown above. Soak in cold water until crisp and curly.

3 Place hot cooked rice in each serving bowl. Arrange pork and sprinkle with sesame seed and scallion. Center long onion shreds.

Hint: This is an easy and spicy version of the popular *Shabushabu* dish.

SICHUAN PICKLE DONBURI

3-4 cups hot cooked rice (see p.6)
⅔ oz (20g) Sichuan pickle
⅔ oz (20g) dried shrimp
½ each, red and green bell pepper
1 Tbsp vegetable oil
COOKING SAUCE
⌈1 tsp soy sauce
│2 tsp sugar
└1 Tbsp sesame oil

Serves: 2

Hint: Do not discard water used to soften the shrimp. It makes a good stock.

1 Cut Sichuan pickle into julienne strips. Slice green pepper thinly lengthwise, and red one into ⅜" (1cm) squares.

2 Rinse dried shrimp briefly, and soak in water until softened (about 30 minutes.)

3 Heat vegetable oil in a frying pan. Stir-fry softened shrimp, then add pepper. Add COOKING SAUCE ingredients and shrimp-soaking water. Stir briskly until the liquid is almost gone.

4 Place hot cooked rice in each serving bowl, and arrange topping.

SPICY GROUND MEAT DONBURI

1 Discard stems of *shiitake* mushrooms and chop finely.

2 In a small bowl, combine *MISO* SAUCE ingredients.

3 Heat vegetable oil in a frying pan, and fry onion and ginger until the aroma is released. Add ground meat and crumble into grains.

4 When the meat turns color, add *miso* sauce and mushrooms. Reduce heat and cook until thickened and glossy. Stir in hot bean paste and sesame oil; turn off heat.

5 Make onion shreds. Cut long onion lengthwise into skins, and remove the core. Shred finely and soak in cold water until crisp and curly; drain.

6 Place hot cooked rice in each serving bowl. Lay lettuce leaves and center ground meat mixture. Garnish with onion shreds.

Hint: Cook ingredients after extracting the aroma of long onion or ginger well.

3-4 cups hot cooked rice
(see p.6)
4 oz(120g) ground pork
½ long onion, minced
1 knob ginger, minced
3 *shiitake* mushrooms
MISO SAUCE
⌈1 Tbsp *akadashi miso*
│1 tsp sugar
│1 tsp soy sauce
│½ Tbsp *sake*
└1⅔ Tbsp water

1 Tbsp vegetable oil
½ tsp toban jang
(hot bean paste)
Dash sesame oil
2"(5cm) long onion
Lettuce leaves

Serves: 2

CURRY DONBURI

1½ cups uncooked rice
[1 Tbsp turmeric
[1 tsp salt
5 oz(150g) ground beef
½ onion, chopped
2 cloves garlic, minced
2 knobs ginger, minced
5oz(150g) spinach, chopped
2 Tbsp sesame oil
½ Tbsp cumin seed
½ lb(200g) canned tomatoes
1 cup chicken stock
1 bay leaf
1 tsp salt
1-2 pods dried red pepper
1 Tbsp garam masala

1 Rinse rice several times and cook with the same amount of water, turmeric and salt, dissolved thoroughly.

2 Heat sesame oil in a saucepan, fry garlic, ginger and onion. Add ground beef and stir-fry until the color turns whitish.

3 Add chopped tomatoes, spinach, chicken stock, bay leaf and salt to the saucepan, and cook over low heat, for about 30 minutes. Lastly add garam masala, and remove bay leaf and red hot pepper.

4 Place cooked rice in each serving bowl, and pour over curry.

Hint: Garnish with fried onion or basil tips, if preferred.

Serves: 2-3

BIBIMBUP

1 Slice beef thinly, then into julienne strips. Combine soy sauce, *mirin*, and grated garlic, and marinate beef strips about 30 minutes.

2 Discard roots from bean sprouts. Cook briefly in salted boiling water; drain and toss with sesame oil and half-ground or chopped sesame seed.

3 Cook spinach briefly in salted boiling water. Plunge into cold water and squeeze out water. Cut up and toss with the mixture of soy sauce, sesame oil, salt and pepper.

4 Shred carrot finely and blanch in salted boiling water; drain and sprinkle with salt, pepper, and half-ground (or chopped) sesame seed.

5 Make thin omelets. In a lightly greased frying pan, pour ¼ - ⅓ of the beaten egg, only to cover the bottom of pan. Remove when set and shred finely. Repeat with the remaining.

6 Place hot cooked rice in each serving bowl. Arrange toppings and *nori*, contrasting colors. Serve with kochu jang , if desired.

3-4 cups hot cooked rice (see p.6)
1 package(3 oz/90g) bean sprouts
[1 tsp sesame oil
[Dash toasted sesame seed
4 oz(120g) spinach
[1 tsp soy sauce
[1 tsp sesame oil
[Salt and pepper
4 oz(120g) lean beef
[1 Tbsp soy sauce
[1 Tbsp *mirin*
[½ tsp grated garlic

1½"(4cm) length carrot
[Salt and pepper
[Dash toasted sesame seed
1 egg, beaten
Nori seaweed, shredded
Pinch salt
1 tsp vegetable oil
Kochu jang(opptional)

Serves: 2

TOFU AND PORK DONBUR

3-4 cups hot cooked rice (see p.6)
1 cake *tofu* （firm type)
3 oz(90g) lean pork
 Salt and pepper
2-3 scallions
1 tsp minced garlic
1 tsp minced ginger
MISO SAUCE
[1½ Tbsp *miso*
 1 Tbsp soy sauce
 1 Tbsp *sake*
 ½ tsp sugar
 Dash pepper
 [½ tsp toban jang (hot bean paste)
1 Tbsp vegetable oil
Dried chili, finely shredded

Serves: 2

1 Cut *tofu* into ⅜"(1cm) cubes and drain as shown, about 10 minutes.

2 Slice pork into thin, bite-sized pieces, and sprinkle with salt and pepper. Cut scallions into 1"(2.5cm) lengths. In a small bowl combine *MISO* SAUCE ingredients.

3 Heat vegetable oil in a frying pan. Fry garlic and ginger until the aroma is released, then add pork and stir-fry.

4 Add *tofu* and *miso* sauce. Cook and stir until the sauce is absorbed.

5 Place hot cooked rice in each serving bowl, and arrange *tofu* mixture. Garnish with shredded chili.

SPICY CHICKEN DONBURI

3-4 cups hot cooked rice (see p.6)
5 oz(150g) chicken thigh
1 bell pepper, cut up
1 tsp curry powder
2 tsp chili sauce
1 Tbsp vegetable oil
Salt and pepper

Serves: 2

1 Cut chicken into bite-sized pieces. Sprinkle with salt and pepper.

2 Grease a frying pan and stir-fry bell pepper. Sprinkle with salt and pepper and set aside.

3 In the same pan, heat remaining oil and sauté chicken pieces until lightly browned. Sprinkle with curry powder and chili sauce, constantly stirring.

4 Place hot cooked rice in each serving bowl. Arrange chicken and pepper on top.

GARLIC OCTOPUS DONBURI

3-4 cups hot cooked rice (see p.6)
4 oz(120g) boiled octopus
½ Japanese-type cucumber
1 clove garlic, minced
¼ long onion, minced
1 pod dried chili pepper
1 Tbsp olive oil
Salt and pepper

Serves: 2

1 Cut octopus into bite-sized pieces. Seed dried chili and slice thinly.

2 Slice cucumber thinly and place in a plastic bag or bowl. Sprinkle with ½ tsp salt and "knead" until supple.

3 Heat olive oil in a frying pan and fry garlic, onion and chili. When the aroma is released, add octopus and stir-fry. Sprinkle in salt and pepper.

4 Place hot cooked rice in each serving bowl, and arrange octopus and pepper over it.

SPICY VERMICELLI DONBURI

3-4 cups hot cooked rice (see p.6)
1¾oz(50g) dried bean vermicelli
3 oz(90g) ground pork
5-6 pods green beans
¼ carrot, shredded
½ tsp minced garlic
½ tsp minced ginger
COOKING SAUCE
⌈3 Tbsp *sake*
 3 Tbsp soy sauce
 1 Tbsp sugar
 1 tsp chicken stock
 1 cup or less boiling water
⌊1 tsp toban jang (hot bean paste)
1 Tbsp sesame oil

Serves: 2

1 Cook bean vermicelli in boiling water about 2 minutes; drain.

2 Cut green beans into about 1"(2.5cm) lengths, and boil briefly, drain. Combine COOKING SAUCE ingredients.

3 Heat sesame oil in a frying pan, and fry garlic and ginger. Add minced pork and stir-fry.

4 Stir in cooking sauce and bring to a boil. Add vermicelli, carrot and green beans. Cook and stir about 5 minutes until the liquid is almost absorbed.

5 Place hot cooked rice in each serving bowl, and transfer the topping onto it.

SPECIAL DINNER DONBURI

CONTENTS

EGG FU YUNG DONBURI p.59
ALLSTAR DONBURI p.59
TRI-COLOR DONBURI p.60
SPRING DONBURI p.60
SASHIMI AND YAM DONBURI
p.60
EEL OMELET DONBURI p.61
AUTUMN HARVEST RICE p.62
PEPPER SHELLFISH DONBURI
p.62
SAUTÉED TUNA DONBURI p.63
MUSHROOM DONBURI p.63

Just a little technique of cutting or preparation goes a long way. You can present the season by cutting ingredients into shapes of flower petals or ginkgo leaves. Arrange these dishes in a lacquer ware or your favorite soup bowl to create a special mood.

EGG FU YUNG DONBURI

3-4 cups hot cooked rice (see p.6)
4 eggs, lightly beaten
  Salt and pepper
¼ long onion, sliced
4 oz(120g) crab meat
1 Tbsp frozen green peas
SWEET SOUR SAUCE
⌈150 ml water
│½ tsp chicken stock
│1 Tbsp soy sauce
│1 Tbsp sugar
│Pinch salt
⌊½ Tbsp rice vinegar
1 Tbsp cornstarch,
  dissolved in ½ Tbsp water
3 Tbsp vegetable oil

Serves: 2

Hint: When wok and oil gets really hot, pour beaten eggs at once and stir with long and slow strokes.

1 Remove cartilage of crab meat, and crumble roughly.

2 In a saucepan, bring SWEET SOUR SAUCE ingredients (except vinegar) to a boil. Add crab meat and peas, and return to a boil. Stir in vinegar and dissolved cornstarch. Turn off heat.

3 Place hot cooked rice in each serving bowl.

4 In a hot wok, heat vegetable oil hot, pour in beaten egg at once. Using a ladle or spatula, pull the egg from the sides of wok to the other side, quickly but carefully several times. When there is little runny egg, transfer half onto the rice. Pour over the sweet sour crab meat sauce.

4

ALLSTAR DONBURI

3-4 cups hot cooked rice (see p.6)
4 oz(120g) thinly sliced pork
2 oz(60g) shrimp, shelled
2 quail eggs, boiled
4 dried *shiitake* mushrooms
2 Chinese cabbage leaves
4-6 pods snow peas, strung
2"(5cm) length carrot
4-6 young corn, canned
1"(2.5cm) long onion
1 small knob ginger
COOKING BROTH
⌈150 ml water
│½ chicken granules
│1 Tbsp *sake*
│1 Tbsp soy sauce
⌊Dash salt, pepper, sugar
1 Tbsp cornstarch,
  dissolved in 2 Tbsp water
1 Tbsp vegetable oil

Serves: 2

1 Soften dried *shiitake* by soaking in lukewarm water about 20 minutes. Cut pork slices into bitesized pieces.

2 Slice carrot lengthwise thinly, and parboil briefly. Mince long onion and ginger. Cut up Chinese cabbage and softened *shiitake*, stems removed.

3 Heat vegetable oil in a frying pan, and fry minced onion and ginger.

4 Add pork and shrimp. Stir-fry briefly and add all vegetables. Continue to stir over high heat until the Chinese cabbage becomes transparent. Add COOKING BROTH.

5 Swirl in dissolved cornstarch and stir quickly. Mound hot cooked rice in each serving bowl, and arrange the topping.

TRI-COLOR DONBURI *(Sanshoku Donburi)*

3-4 cups hot cooked rice (see p.6)
5 oz(150g) ground chicken
Dash minced ginger
1½ Tbsp soy sauce
2 tsp each sugar and *sake*
2 eggs, beaten
1 Tbsp sugar
Pinch salt
4-5 green beans, cooked
Pickled ginger, shredded

Serves: 2

Hint: Stir egg mixture with several chopsticks to make fine crumbles.

1 In a small saucepan, place ground chicken, minced ginger, soy sauce, sugar and *sake*, and combine lightly. Cook and stir over medium heat, until the moisture is evaporated. Adjust the heat and avoid scorching.

2 In another saucepan, blend eggs, sugar and salt. Cook over medium to low heat, stirring constantly with 4 chopsticks or a fork.

3 Cut green beans diagonally into long and thin slices.

4 Place hot cooked rice in each serving bowl, and arrange chicken, egg, and green beans. Garnish with pickled ginger.

SPRING DONBURI

3-4 cups hot cooked rice (see p.6)
2 Tbsp salted cherry blossoms
Kodai sasazuke(miniature skipper pickled with bamboo leaves)
Pink *kamaboko* (steamed fish cake)
Dash *mitsuba*(trefoil)

Serves: 2

1 Slice fish into bite-sized pieces working your knife almost flat, and pressing the fish with your left fingers. Using a cutter, make cherry blossom shapes out of fish cake slices.

2 Rinse cherry blossoms in water briefly and drain. Blanch cut-up *mitsuba* stems in boiling water and drain.

3 Combine fish, fish cake, and cherry blossoms with hot cooked rice and transfer into each serving bowl. Sprinkle with *mitsuba*.

SASHIMI AND YAM DONBURI

3-4 cups hot cooked rice (see p.6)
4 oz(120g) *maguro sashimi*
4 oz(120g) *yama-imo* yam
2 Tbsp *dashi* stock
Wasabi paste
Soy sauce as dip

Serves: 2

1 Cup *maguro sashimi* into bite-sized cubes. Grate yam and thin with *dashi* stock, adding and stirring little by little.

2 Place hot cooked rice in each serving bowl. Place *maguro sashimi* over it and pour in grated yam. Garnish with *wasabi*. Serve with a small bowl of soy sauce.

EEL OMELET DONBURI *(Una-tama Donburi)*

3-4 cups hot cooked rice (see p.6)
1 portion broiled *unagi* (eel)
¼ long onion
4 snow peas, optional
2 eggs, beaten

COOKING BROTH
[200 ml *dashi* stock
1 Tbsp soy sauce
½ Tbsp *mirin*
2 tsp sugar

Serves: 2

1 Cut broiled eel thinly. Cut long onion into ⅜"(1cm) slices.

2 Trim snow peas and cook only briefly in salted boiling water. Slice diagonally into fine strips.

3 Place hot cooked rice in each serving bowl.

4 In a frying pan, place COOKING BROTH ingredients and bring to a boil. Add eel and simmer 5 minutes. Add onion and cook until it is supple. Swirl in beaten eggs and remove from heat when the egg is half set. Transfer onto rice, and garnish with slivered snow peas.

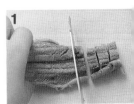

AUTUMN HARVEST RICE

1½ cup long grain rice
2 Tbsp glutenous rice (*mochi-gome*)
⌈4" (10cm) square *kombu* kelp
│1 Tbsp *sake*
⌊1 Tbsp *mirin*
3-4 chestnuts in syrup
1 dozen canned ginkgo nuts
Some boiled shrimp
1 oz(30g) carrot
½ package *shimeji* mushrooms
COOKING BROTH
⌈1 cup *dashi* stock
│Pinch salt
⌊Few drops light soy sauce
¼ package *mitsuba* (trefoil)
Yuzu citron rind, shredded

Serves: 2

1 Rinse both kinds of rice 30 minutes before cooking; drain in a colander and set aside.

2 In a small saucepan, heat 2 cups of water and *kombu.* Just before boiling, remove *kombu* and turn off heat. Pour into rice cooker, and stir in rice, *sake* and *mirin.* Adjust the amount of water to regular level and set to cook.

3 Rinse chestnuts in water to remove syrup. Cut into bite size. Slice carrot and cut out into flower shapes. Trim *shimeji* and divide into segments.

4 In a saucepan, place COOKING BROTH, carrot and mushrooms, and bring to a boil. Cook about 10 minutes until subtly flavored. Cut *mitsuba* into 1"(2.5cm) lengths.

5 When rice is cooked, mix with all the ingredients. Garnish with shredded *yuzu* rind.

Hint: Symbols of autumn are mixed with sticky rice cooked in a delicate broth.

PEPPER SHELLFISH DONBURI

3-4 cups hot cooked rice (see p.6)
1 lb(450g) fresh water clams in shell
⌈2 heap Tbsp *sake*
⌊2 heap Tbsp water
COOKING BROTH
⌈¼ cup shellfish boiling water
│1 Tbsp soy sauce
⌊1 Tbsp *mirin*
Pinch *sansho*(Japanese pepper)
1 egg, beaten with pinch of salt
3-4 scallions, sliced

Serves: 2

1 Cover clams with water and let sit to remove the sand. Rinse clams and cook in *sake* and water until the shells open; take out the flesh.

2 In a small saucepan, bring COOKING BROTH ingredients to a boil and cook until thickened. Stir in clams to hold the flavor. Make thin omelets as shown and shred.

3 Toss hot cooked rice with clams and place in each serving bowl. Top with scallion and shredded omelet.

SAUTÉED TUNA DONBURI

3-4 cups hot cooked rice (see p.6)
4 oz(120g) tuna, thinly sliced
¼ onion, minced
1 Tbsp butter
1 Tbsp soy sauce
Salt and pepper
5-6 *shiso* leaves, shredded

Serves: 2

1 Melt butter in a frying pan and fry minced onion until transparent.

2 Add tuna slices and stir-fry briefly. Stir in soy sauce, salt and pepper.

3 Place hot cooked rice in each serving bowl. Arrange tuna slices and garnish with shredded *shiso* leaves.

Hint: Try this when you have leftover *sashimi*.

MUSHROOM DONBURI

3-4 cups hot cooked rice
(see p.6)
1 package (3½ oz, 100g)
maitake mushroom
½ package(1¾ oz, 50g)
shimeji mushrooms
3-4 *shiitake* mushrooms
Few slices carrot
2 Tbsp *sake*
1 Tbsp soy sauce
Pinch salt
½ Tbsp vegetable oil

Serves: 2

1 Separate *maitake* mushroom into segments. Remove base of *shimeji* mushrooms as shown, and divide into segments. Cut off stems of *shiitake* mushrooms and slice thinly.

2 Cut out ginkgo leaf shapes from carrot slices, and cook briefly in boiling water.

3 Heat vegetable oil in a frying pan. Add mushrooms and sauté over high heat so as not to let the juices out. Season with *sake*, soy sauce and salt.

4 Mound hot cooked rice in each serving bowl, and top with mushrooms and carrot leaves.

Hint: Do not overcook mushrooms. Remove from heat before mushrooms are completely supple.

EASY DONBURI

CONTENTS

CORNED BEEF AND POTATO
DONBURI p.64
FRIED EGGPLANT DONBURI p.65
MOON AND MUSHROOM
DONBURI p.65
FISH AND YAM DONBURI p.65
GRILLED SQUID DONBURI p.66
SCRAMBLED *TOFU* DONBURI
p.66
MIXED SALMON DONBURI p.67
PORK AND POTATO DONBURI
p.67
NATTO DONBURI p.68
EGGPLANT WITH *MISO*
DONBURI p.68
ROASTED PORK DONBURI p.69

Potatoes, eggplant, eggs, mushrooms — using these everyday ingredients or leftovers you can find in the refrigerator, a healthy one-bowl dish can be prepared in no time. Try it with your favorite ingredients.

CORNED BEEF AND POTATO DONBURI

3-4 cups hot cooked rice(see p.6)
4 oz(120 g) canned corned beef
2 small potatoes
¼ onion, minced
2 eggs, beaten
1 Tbsp milk
1 Tbsp butter
Salt and pepper
1 Tbsp vegetable oil
Parsley, minced

Serves: 2

1 Cut potatoes into julienne strips and soak in water to remove harshness.

2 Heat vegetable oil in a frying pan and fry minced onion and drained potato well.

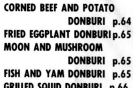

3 Add corned beef and keep stir-frying. Season to taste with salt and pepper.

4 Add milk to beaten eggs, and make fluffy scrambled egg in melted butter.

5 Place hot cooked rice in each serving bowl. Cover with scrambled egg, and then corned beef and potato. Sprinkle with minced parsley.

FRIED EGGPLANT DONBURI

3-4 cups hot cooked rice
  (see p.6)
2 Japanese-type eggplants
3 oz(90g) ground chicken
COOKING BROTH
  ⌈ ½ cup *dashi* stock
   2 Tbsp soy sauce
   1Tbsp *sake*
  ⌊ 1 tsp sugar
1 tsp cornstarch,
  dissolved in 2 tsp water
Vegetable oil for deep-frying
Shiso(perilla) leaves, optional

Serves: 2

Note: Delicate chicken sauce enhances the juicy eggplant.

1 Discard caps of eggplants and cut lengthwise into 5 or 6. Soak in water to remove harshness for 5 minutes and drain. Heat vegetable oil to medium hot and deep-fry eggplant. Drain and pat with kitchen towel to absorb excess oil.

2 In a small saucepan, bring COOKING BROTH ingredients to a boil. Add ground chicken, and stir to crumble. When chicken is done, stir in dissolved cornstarch until the liquid becomes clear.

3 Place hot cooked rice in each serving bowl. Arrange fried eggplant and drizzle chicken sauce on top. Garnish with herb of your choice.

MOON AND MUSHROOM DONBURI

3-4 cups hot cooked rice(see p.6)
2 fresh eggs
½ package *shimeji* mushrooms
1 package *enokidake* mushrooms
COOKING BROTH
  ⌈ ¾ cup *dashi* stock
   2 Tbsp *mirin*
   2 Tbsp soy sauce
  ⌊ 1 tsp ginger juice
½ tsp cornstarch,
  dissolved in 3 tsp water
Vegetable oil for greasing

Serves: 2

1 Heat oil in a frying pan and fry one egg until half cooked.

2 Trim *shimeji* mushrooms and separate into segments. Cut off root ends of *enokidake* mushrooms.

3 In a small saucepan, bring COOKING BROTH ingredients to a boil. Add mushrooms and cook briefly just until they absorb the flavor. Stir in dissolved cornstarch quickly and turn off heat.

4 Place hot cooked rice in a serving bowl. Center the fried egg and arrange mushroom sauce around it.

Note: Break egg yolk and blend with mushrooms and rice as you eat.

FISH AND YAM DONBURI

3-4 cups hot cooked rice (see p.6)
2 dried horse mackerel or salmon
4 oz(120 g) *yama-imo* yam
Few drops vinegar
2 Tbsp *dashi* stock
½ sheet *nori* seaweed, shredded
Dab of *wasabi* paste

Serves: 2

1 Grill dried fish and break into flakes.

2 Peel *yamato-imo* yam and soak in vinegared water for 5 minutes. Grate in a grinding bowl as shown. Thin with *dashi* stock, added little at a time.

3 Place hot cooked rice in each serving bowl. Arrange flaked fish over it and pour grated yam. Top with *nori* seaweed and *wasabi*.

Note: No seasonings are necessary as the dried fish has enough saltiness.

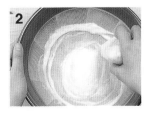

3-4 cups hot cooked rice (see p.6)
1 semi-dried squid (ichiya-boshi)
MARINADE
[3 Tbsp soy sauce
3 Tbsp mirin
1 tsp ginger juice
4-6 shiso leaves
2 tsp grated ginger

Serves: 2

1 Remove skin of the squid, and make criss-cross scores diagonally all over the surface. Soak in MARINADE for 20 minutes.

2 Grill both sides of drained squid. Slice lengthwise into bite size pieces.

3 Place hot cooked rice in each serving bowl. Lay 2-3 shiso leaves and arrange squid pieces over it. Top with grated ginger.

Hint: If "ichiya-boshi" is unavailable, wrap squid with dehydrating film overnight.

GRILLED SQUID DONBURI

SCRAMBLED *TOFU* DONBURI

3-4 cups hot cooked rice (see p.6)
1-2 bok choy greens
½ cake tofu (firm type)
1 egg, beaten
1 Tbsp sesame oil
2 Tbsp sugar
2 Tbsp soy sauce

Serves: 2

1 Drain tofu and lay on a flat surface. Place a light weight such as a dish filled with water. Let stand for 30 minutes.

2 Cook bok choy in boiling water; drain and cut up.

3 Heat sesame oil in a wok, and stir-fry bok choy. Add tofu, breaking up into crumbles. Cook and stir until the liquid evaporates. Season to taste with sugar and soy sauce. Swirl in beaten egg, and toss lightly.

4 Serve over hot cooked rice.

Hint: Wrap tofu with kitchen towel before putting a weight, for effective draining.

MIXED SALMON DONBURI

3-4 cups hot cooked rice (see p.6)
1 fillet salted salmon
½ Japanese-type cucumber
 Salt to knead
5-6 *shiso* leaves, shredded
2 slices lemon
Lemon juice
1 Tbsp toasted white sesame seeds

Serves: 2

1 Grill or microwave salted salmon and remove skin and bones. Break the flesh into flakes.

2 Slice cucumber thinly and diagonally. Then cut the slices into match sticks. Sprinkle with salt and "knead" until supple. Squeeze out moisture.

3 In a large bowl, place hot cooked rice and sprinkle with lemon juice. Toss rice with salmon, cucumber and sesame seeds.

4 Place the mixed rice in each serving bowl and top with *shiso* leaves and lemon slices.

3-4 cups hot cooked rice (see p.6)
1 small potato
4 oz(120 g) thinly sliced pork
½ package (3⅓oz, 100g)yam noodles(*shirataki*)
¼ onion
1 Tbsp frozen green peas
COOKING BROTH
⌈1 cup *dashi* stock
 2 Tbsp *sake*
 2 Tbsp *mirin*
⌊2 Tbsp sugar
3 Tbsp soy sauce
2 Tbsp vegetable oil

Serves: 2

1 Peel potato and cut into bite-size pieces. Soak in water and drain.

2 Boil yam noodles about 2 minutes; drain and cut up. Cut onion into wedges.

3 Heat vegetable oil in a frying pan and sauté pork slices. Add potato and stir-fry briefly. Add *dashi* stock and bring to a boil. Skim away the floating scum. Add *sake*, *mirin* and sugar, and simmer 5-6 minutes putting a drop lid to keep the ingredients in the broth.

4 Add yam noodles and soy sauce. Continue to simmer until the potato is tender and absorbs the flavor. Add green peas.

5 Place hot cooked rice in each serving bowl. Arrange pork and potato on it.

PORK AND POTATO DONBURI
(*Nikujaga Donburi*)

NATTO DONBURI

3-4 cups *sushi* rice (see p.12)
1 portion *natto* (3 oz /90g)
1 Tbsp soy sauce
3-4 scallions, sliced
1 sheet *nori* seaweed, shredded
2 egg yolks

Serves: 2

1 Toss steaming rice with combined *sushi* vinegar, gently but throughly. Fluff rice and cool with a fan or cardboard.

2 Cut up *natto* only roughly, and combine with soy sauce and scallion. Stir until smooth and sticky.

3 Place *sushi* rice in each serving bowl. Lay *natto* mixture in the center. Frame it with shredded *nori*. Make a hollow in the center and drop in egg yolk.

Hint: Mix in egg yolk with *natto* as you eat. Egg yolk makes the *natto* taste milder and richer.

EGGPLANT WITH *MISO* DONBURI

3-4 cups hot cooked rice (see p.6)
2 Japanese-type eggplants
3 pods sweet pepper or okura
SEASONING
⎡1 ½ Tbsp *miso*
⎢1 Tbsp sugar
⎢1 Tbsp *sake*
⎣Dash ginger juice
1 Tbsp vegetable oil
7-spice powder *(shichimi)*

Serves: 2

1 Slice eggplants into rounds and soak in water for 5 minutes to remove harshness. Slice pepper pods.

2 Combine all SEASONING ingredients.

3 Heat oil in a frying pan and sauté eggplant slices turning once. Add pepper and stir-fry briefly. Add combined seasoning and continue to stir.

4 Place hot cooked rice in each serving bowl. Arrange eggplant and pepper slices on top and sprinkle 7-spice powder, if desired.

ROASTED PORK DONBURI *(Yakibuta Donburi)*

3-4 cups hot cooked rice (see p.6)
4 oz(120g) roasted pork(*yakibuta*)
1-2 bok choy greens
Dash Sichuan pickle
2 tsp sesame oil
1 tsp soy sauce
1 tsp *sake*
SAUCE
⎡ 2⅓ Tbsp soy sauce
⎢ 1 Tbsp sugar
⎣ ⅓ Tbsp each *mirin*, *sake* and *miso*

Serves: 2

Note: Flavorful mixed rice made easy with shop-bought roast pork (*yakibuta*).

1 Cut Sichuan pickle into ¼" (6mm) squares. Slice *yakibuta* into ¼" (6mm) thicknesses and save some for topping. Cut the remaining slices into dices. Cut up bok choy greens as well.

2 Heat sesame oil in a frying pan, and stir-fry all cut-up ingredients except large slices. As soon as the bok choy becomes supple, stir in *sake* and soy sauce.

3 In a small saucepan, bring SAUCE ingredients to a boil.

4 In a large bowl, mix hot rice with pork mixture. Transfer into each serving bowl, and place fanned-out pork slices. Pour sauce over them and serve.

Hint: Do not overcook greens as it spoils the crispness.

COLORFUL DONBURI FOR KIDS

CONTENTS

TUNA AND EGG DONBURI p.71

OMELET DONBURI p.71

CARROT RICE p.72

SUSHI MELANGE DONBURI p.73

BACON AND EGG DONBURI
p.73

TRI-COLOR MIXED RICE p.74

DIM SUM (SIU MAI) DONBURI
p.74

MIXED SEAFOOD DONBURI
p.75

Make your children home-made, nourishing, and stuffing one-bowl meals appetizingly presented. Children love bright colors and playful shapes, and will try them even if the dishes are new to them. Think of attractive combinations in colors and nutrition.

TUNA AND EGG DONBURI

2-3 cups hot cooked rice (see p.6)
3 oz(90g) canned tuna
2 Tbsp canned green peas
3 eggs, beaten
1 Tbsp soy sauce
1 Tbsp *mirin*
Pinch sugar, salt and pepper
3 Tbsp butter

Serves: 2

1 Drain canned tuna and break into flakes (on a kitchen towel as shown).

2 Melt 1 Tbsp butter in a small saucepan, and add  tuna and peas. Stir-fry briefly over medium heat. Add soy sauce and *mirin*. Cook and stir 5-6 minutes until the liquid is absorbed.

Ordinary scrambled eggs make an attractive meal with canned tuna and peas.

3 In a bowl, combine beaten eggs, sugar, salt and pepper.

4 Heat a frying pan and melt remaining butter. Add egg mixture and stir with long strokes to make fluffy scrambled egg.

5 Place hot cooked rice in each serving bowl. Cover with scrambled egg, and center with tuna mixture.

OMELET DONBURI

Children's No.1 favorite, served in a bowl.

1 Heat 1 tsp oil in a frying pan, and fry chopped onion until clear. Add ground meat and stir-fry, crumbling well.

2 Stir in cooked rice and season with salt, pepper and ketchup. Transfer into each serving bowl.

3 Season beaten egg with salt and pepper, and pour into the frying pan greased with the remaining oil. Stir over low heat, until the egg is nearly set, but not well done. Slide this thin omelet onto the rice. Make a crisscross cut in the center and decorate with ketchup and parsley.

2-3 cups cooked rice(see p.6)
4 oz(120g) ground pork
½ small onion, chopped
2 eggs, beaten
Salt and pepper

3 Tbsp ketchup
2 tsp vegetable oil
Parsley, optional

Serves: 2

Unexpectedly delicious dish with fried and seasoned carrot.

CARROT RICE

1½ cups uncooked rice
1 small carrot
2-3 pods snow peas
6 slices *kamaboko* (steamed fish cake)
1 egg, beaten
⌈1 tsp sugar
⌊Pinch salt
Vegetable oil
SEASONING
⌈1 Tbsp *sake*
⎪½ Tbsp soy sauce
⎪½ Tbsp *mirin*
⌊½ tsp salt

Serves: 4

1 Place rinsed rice in rice cooker, and start cooking.

2 Peel carrot and cut into two. Shred one half and cut out shapes from the other half, using a cooker cutter. Also cut out shapes from *kamaboko*.

3 Cook snow peas and carrot shapes briefly in boiling water.

4 Combine beaten egg with sugar and salt. Grease frying pan and make scramble egg, set aside.

5 Heat vegetable oil in the frying pan, and sauté shredded carrot until supple. Add SEASONING ingredients and stir until liquid is absorbed.

6 When the rice is in the final, steaming process, add the seasoned carrot and cover immediately. Let steam about 10 minutes. Toss to fluff the rice and mix with the carrot.

7 Place in each serving bowl, and decorate with scrambled egg, shredded snow peas, carrot shapes and fish cake.

Hint: Make a carrot decoration using a miniature carrot and a sprig of parsley.

SUSHI MELANGE DONBURI

2 cups hot cooked rice (see p.6)
2 portions *gomokuzushi-no-moto*
1 egg, beaten
2 Tbsp *denbu* (fish flakes)
5-6 pods snow peas
Salt

Serves: 2

1 Toss hot cooked rice with *gomoku-zushi* no moto, evenly.

2 Boil snow peas briefly and cut out shapes using a cookie cutter.

3 Make 2-3 thin omelets with beaten egg and cut out using a cutter.

4 Mound mixed *sushi* rice in each serving bowl, and decorate with *denbu*, omelet and snow peas.

Note: *Gomokuzushi-no-moto* is available in retort pouch, including seasoned vegetables and rice vinegar to mix with plain hot rice.

Quick and savory vegetable *sushi*, using a prepared mix.

BACON AND EGG DONBURI

2-3 cups hot cooked rice
   (see p.6)
4 slices bacon
2 eggs
¼ head broccoli
Pinch salt

Serves: 2

1 Separate broccoli into florets and cook in salty boiling water just until tender but not soggy.

2 Cut bacon into bite-size pieces. Fry bacon in a frying pan until crisp. Remove excess oil with a kitchen towel. Make one portion each: arrange half amount of bacon in the frying pan, and drop a whole egg in the center. Cover and cook until half cooked.

3 Place hot cooked rice in each serving bowl. Transfer fried egg with bacon onto it, and add broccoli florets.

No special skill is needed to make this balanced meal.

TRI-COLOR MIXED RICE

2-3 cups hot cooked rice (see p.6)
3 Tbsp canned whole corn
2 Tbsp green peas, thawed
2 slices fully cooked ham
1 tsp butter
Salt and pepper

Serves: 2

1 Drain corn while cutting ham into ⅜"(1cm) squares.

2 Melt butter in a frying pan, and fry corn, ham and green peas only briefly. Season to taste, adding some extra salt and pepper for the rice.

3 Mix hot cooked rice and cooked ingredients, so as not to break the grains. Transfer into each serving bowl.

This kids' favorite pleases the eye and palate.

DIM SUM(SIU MAI)DONBURI

Try with meatballs or leftover hambergers.

2-3 cups hot cooked rice (see p.6)
6 bought siu mai dumplings
½ onion, sliced
3-4 *shiitake* mushrooms
Thawed green peas
2 eggs, lightly beaten
COOKING BROTH
[1 Tbsp each sugar, *sake*, soy sauce and *mirin*
[200ml *dashi* stock

Serves: 2

1 Cut each dumpling in half or into bite-size pieces.

2 Trim stems from *shiitake* mushrooms and slice thinly. Blanch green peas in boiling water and drain.

3 In a small saucepan bring COOKING BROTH to a boil. Add onion and mushrooms. Cook about 3 minutes, and add siu mai dumplings. Cook a further 5 minutes and sprinkle with green peas.

4 Swirl in beaten egg, and place a lid. Simmer over low heat until the egg is almost set.

5 Place hot cooked rice in each serving bowl, and transfer siu mai mixture onto it.

MIXED SEAFOOD DONBURI

2-3 cups hot cooked rice (see p.6)
4 oz(120g) frozen seafood mix
1 ½"(4cm) carrot, sliced
Snow peas
1 Tbsp dried black fungus
SEASONING
⌈ ½ Tbsp soy sauce
| 1 Tbsp *sake*
| Pinch sugar
| Few drops ginger juice
| 200ml water
| ½ tsp chicken granules
⌊ Salt and pepper
½ Tbsp cornstarch
1 Tbsp vegetable oil

Serves: 2

1 Blanch frozen seafood mix in boiling water and drain. Soak dried black fungus in hot water until softened.

2 Cook carrot in boiling water and cut into various shapes using cookie cutters.

3 String snow peas and blanch in boiling water. Drain and cut into shapes.

4 Heat vegetable oil in a frying pan, and stir-fry seafood, softened fungus and vegetables briefly. Stir in SEASONING. Dissolve cornstarch in double amount of water and stir in to thicken the sauce.

5 Place hot cooked rice in each serving bowl, and transfer the topping onto it.

A good strategy for children who dislike vegetables.

LOW CALORIE DONBURI

CONTENTS

COD ROE DONBURI p.77
PEPPER AND SARDINE
                DONBURI p.77
FRIED RICE WITH PICKLED
                PLUMS p.77
SPICY YAM CAKE DONBURI
                p.78
FLAKED SALMON DONBURI
                p.78
CELERY AND PICKLE DONBURI
                p.79
FISH CAKE DONBURI p.79
SALAD DONBURI p.80
WINTER MELON AND MEAT
                SAUCE DONBURI p.80
RICE PORRIDGE WITH SWEET
                POTATO p.81
ASSORTED PICKLE DONBURI
                p.81

Here is an inventive array of one-bowl dishes that are light in both flavors and calories. Use as much vegetables and *konnyaku* (non-calorie yam cake) as you can in everyday meals. Try to take in less oil by using non-stick pots and pans, and adopt an "illusional effect" about the volume by serving a heap in a small bowl.

COD ROE DONBURI

3-4 cups hot cooked rice (see p.6)
4 Tbsp frozen green peas
1 bag salted cod roe (*tarako*)
1 package (7 oz/ 200g) yam noodles (*shirataki*)
COOKING BROTH
[100ml *dashi* stock
½ Tbsp *sake* and *mirin*
2 Tbsp sugar
1 Tbsp soy sauce
Pinch salt
Kinome (*sansho* sprout), optional

Serves: 2

Hint: Enjoy the resilient texture and delicate flavor of this unusual topping.

1 Cook salted cod roe in boiling water briefly. Peel and crumble.

2 Cook yam noodles in boiling water 2-3 minutes, drain and cut up.

3 In salted boiling water, cook green peas briefly and drain.

2

4 In a small saucepan, bring COOKING BROTH to a boil. Add yam noodles and cook for 2-3 minutes.

5 Add crumbled cod roe and cook over low heat until the liquid is absorbed.

6 Mix hot cooked rice with green peas and place in each serving bowl. Spread yam noodle mixture over it and garnish with *kinome*, if preferred.

PEPPER AND SARDINE DONBURI

3-4 cups hot cooked rice
    (see p.6)
3 small bell peppers
1 oz(30g) dried baby sardine
1 Tbsp sesame oil
SEASONING
[1 Tbsp soy sauce
1 Tbsp *mirin*
1 Tbsp *sake*

Serves: 2

1 Halve bell peppers lengthwise, and remove seeds and caps. Slice as thinly as possible. In a small bowl, combine SEASONING ingredients.

2 Heat sesame oil in a frying pan, and fry baby sardine briefly. Add pepper and stir in the combined seasoning. Cook until the liquid evaporates.

2

3 Place hot cooked rice in each serving bowl, and mound the topping.

FRIED RICE WITH PICKLED PLUMS

3-4 cups cooked rice
    (see p.6)
2 pickled plums (*umeboshi*)
¼ cup dried baby sardine
½ clove garlic
2 tsp soy sauce
Vegetable oil for greasing
10 *shiso* (perilla) leaves

Serves: 2

1 Remove stones from pickled plums and mince the fruit. Shred *shiso* leaves. Mince garlic.

2 Lightly grease a heated frying pan, and fry garlic until the aroma is released. Add pickled plum, baby sardines and rice. Stir-fry over high heat until the rice grains are separated. Drizzle soy sauce into the sides of the pan.

3 Transfer into each serving bowl, and garnish with shredded *shiso* leaves.

Hint: Unexpectedly matching combination of garlic and pickled plums.

SPICY YAM CAKE DONBURI

3-4 cups hot cooked rice (see p.6)
1 cake *konnyaku*(yam cake)
2"(5cm) long onion
1 dried red hot pepper
SEASONING
⎡½ Tbsp sugar
⎢1 Tbsp *sake*
⎢½ Tbsp *mirin*
⎣1 Tbsp soy sauce
1 Tbsp vegetable oil

Serves: 2

Note: *Konnyaku*(yam cake) is known as a non-calorie diet food and also as a "sweeper" of your intestines whereas capsaicin burns up the fat in your body. The golden combination for diet, hot pepper and *konnyaku*.

1 Boil *konnyaku*(yam cake) 2-3 minutes. Drain and cut into bite-size pieces using a spoon as shown. This way the cake has rough and larger surfaces to absorb flavors.

2 Make onion shreds: Discard the core of the long onion, and shred lengthwise as fine as possible. Soak in cold water until crisp.

3 Seed pepper and slice thinly. Heat oil in a frying pan and fry yam cake and pepper well over medium heat. Add SEASONING and stir constantly until the liquid is evaporated.

4 Place hot cooked rice in each serving bowl. Arrange yam cake on it and top with drained onion shreds.

FLAKED SALMON DONBURI

3-4 cups *sushi* rice(see p.12)
¼ jar salmon flakes (1 oz/30g)
8 stalks *mitsuba*(trefoil)

2 *myoga* sprouts
1 Tbsp toasted sesame seed

Serves: 2

1 Crumble salmon for even mixing.

2 Blanch *mitsuba* in boiling water, and cut into 1"(2.5cm) lengths.

3 Slice *myoga* thinly and soak in water for 5 minutes to remove harshness.

4 In a large bowl, mix *sushi* rice, salmon, *mitsuba*, and *myoga*. Do not break the grains of rice and work with a wooden spatula in a "cutting" motion.

5 Transfer into each serving bowl, and sprinkle with a thick slice of *myoga*, *mitsuba*, and toasted sesame seed.

Hint: Substitute *myoga* with spring onion or coriander.

CELERY AND PICKLE DONBURI

3-4 cups hot cooked rice (see p.6)
¼ cake *konnyaku*(yam cake)
 2 tsp soy sauce
1 oz(30g) Sichuan pickle
1"(2.5cm) long onion or scallion
¼ stalk celery
1 tsp sesame oil
Dash pepper
Mitsuba (trefoil) or coriander

Serves: 2

1 Cook *konnyaku*(yam cake) in boiling water 2-3 minutes and drain.

2 Cut all ingredients except long onion into thin rectangles. Cut long onion into julienne strips.

3 In a saucepan, stir and cook yam cake without oil for about 2 minutes. Stir in soy sauce. Add sesame oil, Sichuan pickle, long onion and celery. Stir-fry well and sprinkle on pepper.

4 Place hot cooked rice in each serving bowl, and arrange the topping.
Garnish with a *mitsuba* or coriander sprig.

3

FISH CAKE DONBURI

3-4 cups hot cooked rice (see p.6)
1 bunch *komatsuna* greens (about 4 oz/100g)
2"(5cm) *kamaboko* (steamsd fish cake)
Pinch salt
SEASONING
⌈1 Tbsp soy sauce
│1 Tbsp *dashi* stock
│½ tsp hot mustard paste
⌊Juice of 1 *sudachi* or lime

Serves: 2

1 Cook *komatsuna* greens in salted boiling water briefly. Plunge into cold water and drain.

2 Cut *kamaboko* fish cake into thin rectangles. Cut *komatsuna* accordingly.

3 In a bowl, combine SEASONING and mix with *kamaboko and* greens.

4 Place hot cooked rice in each serving bowl, and put *kamaboko* mixture on top.

SALAD DONBURI

3-4 cups cooked rice (see p.6)
1 Japanese-type cucumber
2"(5cm) carrot
2 lettuce leaves
4 sticks Krabmeat
3 cherry tomatoes
French dressing

Serves: 2

1 Cut cucumber, carrot and lettuce into julienne strips. Tear Krabmeat into fine strips. Cut each cherry tomato into 6 wedges.

2 In a bowl, toss all vegetables with French dressing.

3 Place cooked rice and top with the tossed salad.

Hint: Use a non-oil dressing.

WINTER MELON AND MEAT SAUCE DONBURI

3-4 cups hot cooked rice (see p.6)
⅛ winter melon (1 lb/450g)
1 cup *dashi* stock
2 Tbsp *sake*
1 Tbsp *mirin*

1 Tbsp light soy sauce
3 oz(90g) ground pork
½ Tbsp cornstarch, dissolved in 1 Tbsp water
1 tsp ginger juice

Serves: 2

1 Cut winter melon into 1"(2.5cm) cubes as shown, and peel partially. Score onto the skin.

2 Parboil winter melon in ample boiling water for about 10 minutes.

3 In a saucepan, bring to a boil: *dashi* stock, *sake*, *mirin* and light soy sauce. Add water melon and simmer about 20 minutes. Remove water melon.

4 To the remaining broth, add ground pork and stir to crumble. When the meat is cooked, stir in ginger juice and dissolved cornstarch. When the sauce is thickened, remove from heat.

5 Place hot cooked rice in each serving bowl. Arrange water melon pieces and pour over meat sauce.

RICE PORRIDGE WITH SWEET POTATO *(Imo-gayu)*

1½ cups cooked rice (see p.6)
2-3 cups water
1⅓oz(40g) sweet potato
1 cup *dashi* stock
Pinch salt
1 tsp toasted sesame seeds

Serves: 2

1 Peel sweet potato thickly and cut into ⅜"(1cm) dices and soak in water about 10 minutes to remove harshness. Cook in *dashi* stock until tender.

2 Rinse cooked rice so as to remove stickiness. Boil with the measured water about 5 minutes. Add salt and sweet potato. Transfer into each serving bowl and sprinkle with sesame seeds.

Hint: Cook sweet potato until a skewer pierces through smoothly.

ASSORTED PICKLE DONBURI *(Kakuya Donburi)*

3-4 cups hot cooked rice (see p.6)
2 Tbsp chopped *shiba-zuke* pickle
2 Tbsp chopped *nozawana* pickle
2 Tbsp chopped *takuan* pickle
2 Tbsp toasted sesame seeds
1 sheet *nori* seaweed
½ salted cod roe (*tarako*)
1 tsp *sake*

Serves: 2

1 Remove the filmy skin of cod roe. Crumble and sprinkle with *sake* as shown.

2 Place hot cooked rice in each serving bowl. Sprinkle with *nori* and sesame seeds.

3 Arrange pickles in a pinwheel fashion and mound cod roe in the center.

Note: *Kakuya* stands for cut-up pickles.

Calcium-rich Seafood Donburi

CONTENTS

OIL SARDINE DONBURI p.83
BUTTERED SCALLOP DONBURI
                        p.83
SALMON STEAK DONBURI p.84
CURRIED SARDINE DONBURI
                        p.84
SWEET SOUR SWORDFISH
              DONBURI p.85
GARLIC SCALLOP DONBURI p.86
SALMON CHEESE DONBURI p.87
CLAM DONBURI p.87
TERIYAKI SARDINE DONBURI
                        p.88

Fish and shellfish are important source of calcium for Japanese. It is better to take in calcium through everyday meal rather than tablets. When you plan menus, try to include seafood as often as possible so as not to worry about osteoporosis! The recipes in this section introduces richly seasoned, savory toppings perfect for plain rice.

OIL SARDINE DONBURI

3-4 cups hot cooked rice (see p.6)
2 small cans sardine in oil
SEASONING
[1½ Tbsp each soy sauce, *sake*, *mirin*
[1 tsp sugar
½ knob ginger root
Daikon sprouts, optional
Lemon juice

Serves: 2

1 Drain sardine and place on a kitchen towel to remove excess oil.

2 Discard roots of *daikon* sprouts and cut up. Shred ginger root.

3 In a frying pan, bring SEASONING ingredients to a boil and lay sardine. Simmer until the sauce is thickened to half, as shown.

4 Place hot cooked rice in each serving bowl. Pour over remaining sauce from the frying pan, and arrange sardine. Garnish with ginger and *daikon* sprouts. Sprinkle with lemon juice.

BUTTERED SCALLOP DONBURI

1 Sprinkle scallops with *sake* and salt. Let stand 10 minutes. Shred *shiso* leaves finely.

2 Melt butter in a frying pan, and sauté both sides of scallops until golden brown.

3 Combine soy sauce and *mirin*, and drizzle in from the sides of the pan so as to evaporate quicker.

4 Place hot cooked rice in each serving bowl. Arrange scallops and pour over remaining sauce. Garnish with shredded *shiso* leaves.

3-4 cups hot cooked rice
  (see p.6)
1-1½ dozen small scallops
1 Tbsp *sake*
Pinch salt
1 Tbsp butter
3 Tbsp soy sauce
1 Tbsp *mirin*
4-5 *shiso*(perrila) leaves

Serves: 2

Note: Store fresh scallops in the freezer so you can cook this in no time.

SALMON STEAK DONBURI

3-4 cups hot cooked rice (see p.6)
2 salmon fillets
⎡Salt and pepper
⎣All-purpose flour for dusting
2 Tbsp butter
1 Tbsp soy sauce
5-6 drops lemon juice
6 pods snow peas
Toasted sesame seeds
Parsley or coriander, minced
2 slices lemon

Serves: 2

Hint: Tenderly grilled salmon goes with plain rice very well.

1 Sprinkle salmon fillets with salt and pepper. Dust lightly with flour. Blanch snow peas in salty boiling water.

2 Melt butter in a frying pan and sauté salmon fillets, turning once.

3 Drizzle in soy sauce from the sides of the pan, as shown, to release the moisture quickly. Sprinkle with lemon juice.

3

4 Place hot cooked rice in each serving bowl. Sprinkle toasted sesame seeds over the rice and arrange salmon cut into several pieces, alternating with a slice of lemon. Place snow peas and minced parsley.

CURRIED SARDINE DONBURI

3-4 cups hot cooked rice (see p.6)
4 small sardine
Salt and pepper
2 Tbsp curry powder
1 Tbsp all-purpose flour
1 Tbsp vegetable oil
Parsley, minced

Serves: 2

1 Discard heads and insides of sardine. Split open sardine by inserting your thumb from the belly side and working it along the backbone. Remove backbone. Sprinkle with salt and pepper.

2 Mix curry powder and all-purpose flour. Dust sardine with this mixture.

3 Heat vegetable oil in a frying pan. Sauté sardine, skin side up. Turn over when lightly browned.

4 Place hot cooked rice in each serving bowl. Lay cooked sardine and sprinkle with minced parsley.

3

SWEET SOUR SWORDFISH DONBURI

3-4 cups hot cooked rice (see p.6)
2 fillets swordfish
⌈Salt and pepper
⌊Cornstarch for dusting
Vegetable oil for deep-frying
2-3 *shiitake* mushrooms
1 ½"(4cm) carrot
1 slice canned pineapple
2 tbsp canned green peas
SWEET SOUR SAUCE
⌈1 Tbsp each rice vinegar, sugar and
⌊ soy sauce
⌊3 Tbsp water
½ Tbsp cornstarch
1 Tbsp vegetable oil

Serves: 2

Hint: Perfect teaming of plain white-meat fish and flavorful vegetable sauce.

1 Make crisscross scores over fish fillet as shown left. Dust lightly with cornstarch. Deep-fry until golden in vegetable oil and drain.

2 Slice *shiitake* mushrooms and carrot thinly. Using a cookie cutter, cut out shapes from carrot slices. Cut up pineapple.

3 In a small bowl, combine SWEET SOUR SAUCE ingredients. Heat vegetable oil in a frying pan, and stir-fry mushrooms, carrot and pineapple slices. Pour over the sauce and bring to a boil. Cook for 3 minutes.

4 Stir in cornstarch dissolved in double amount of water and add green peas.

5 Place hot cooked rice in each serving bowl. Lay fried fish and pour over the sauce.

GARLIC SCALLOP DONBURI

3-4 cups hot cooked rice (see p.6)
2 oz(60g) spinach
⌈Vegetable oil
⌊Salt and pepper
6 large, boiled scallops
 1 clove garlic, minced
2 Tbsp butter
2 Tbsp white wine
1 Tbsp soy sauce
Parsley, minced

Serves: 2

Hint: Pat dry scallops before cooking and do not overcook them.

1 Cut up spinach and sauté in small amount of vegetable oil. Sprinkle with salt and pepper. Remove from the pan and set aside.

2 Heat vegetable oil in the same pan, and add minced garlic. When the aroma is released, sauté scallops; remove and set aside.

3 In the same pan, heat wine and soy sauce. Stir in butter. Continue to cook just until the butter melts.

1

4 Place hot cooked rice in each serving bowl. Cover the rice with spinach and top with scallops. Sprinkle with minced parsley.

SALMON CHEESE DONBURI

3-4 cups hot cooked rice (see p.6)
2 fillets fresh salmon
[Salt and pepper
[All-purpose flour for dusting
1 Tbsp vegetable oil
1 Tbsp butter
2 oz(60g) shredded mozzarella cheese
½ Tbsp white wine
1 Tbsp milk
Parsley, minced

Serves: 2

1 Sprinkle salmon fillets with salt and pepper. Heat vegetable oil in a frying pan, and saute salmon over medium heat until golden on both sides. Remove from the pan.

2 In the same pan, melt butter and add cheese, wine and milk. Cook and stir over low heat until the mixture has an even texture.

3 Place hot cooked rice in each serving bowl. Lay sautéed salmon and pour over cheese sauce. Garnish with minced parsley.

Hint: Mix the cheese sauce with steaming rice when eating.

3-4 cups hot cooked rice
   (see p.6)
10 large clams
 2 Tbsp *sake*
150 ml water
3 Tbsp *sake*
1 Tbsp soy sauce
1 Tbsp *mirin*
2 eggs
 Pinch sugar and salt
Nori seaweed, shredded
Scallion

Serves: 2

Hint: Use canned clams boiled down with seasonings.

1 Clean clams and sprinkle with *sake*.

2 In a heated frying pan, place clams with *sake*. Cover and steam over high heat. Take out opened shells immediately and remove the flesh.

3 In a saucepan, bring water, *sake*, soy sauce and *mirin* to a boil. Add clams and return to boil. Cook for 1-2 minutes over low heat. Turn off heat and allow to cool so the clams absorb the flavors.

4 Make thin omelets. Combine eggs with sugar and salt. In lightly greased frying pan, pour ⅓ of egg mixture to cover the bottom of pan. Remove when set, and repeat with the remainder. Layer and roll the omelets and shred finely.

5 Place hot cooked rice in each serving bowl. Cover with shredded *nori*.

CLAM DONBURI

Arrange shredded omelet and top with clams. Sprinkle sliced scallions.

3-4 cups hot cooked rice (see p.6)
4 fresh sardine
1 ½ Tbsp cornstarch
1 Tbsp vegetable oil
TERIYAKI SAUCE
⎡1 Tbsp soy sauce
⎢1 Tbsp sugar
⎢1 Tbsp *mirin*
⎣½ Tbsp *sake*
Mitsuba(trefoil) or coriander
7-spice powder, optional

Serves: 2

TERIYAKI SARDINE DONBURI

1

1 Remove heads and insides of sardine. Rinse under running water; drain. Insert your thumb into belly side and work along the backbone to open flat. Remove bones and dust with cornstarch.

2 Heat vegetable oil in a frying pan, and cook sardine, skin side up. Turn over to cook the other side. Remove from the pan.

In the same pan, bring *TERIYAKI* SAUCE to a boil and return the sardine. Shake the pan so the fish is coated evenly with the sauce.

3 Place hot cooked rice in each serving bowl. Lay 2 fillets of sardine. Garnish with *mitsuba*, blanched in boiling water. Serve with 7-spice powder, if desired.

THE NUTRITIONAL VALUE OF FISH

The fat in fish is composed of poly-unsaturated fatty acids and much less cholesterol than meats. Besides, it is proved that docosahexaenoic acid (DHA) which is contained in sardine, tuna, mackerel or bonito, helps to reduce cholesterol and prevents hardening of the arteries.

INDEX

abura-age →see Soybean products
ABURA-AGE DONBURI, 34
ALLSTAR DONBURI, 59
ASSORTED PICKLE DONBURI, 81
ASSORTED SASHIMI DONBURI, 16
atsu-age →see Soybean products
ATSU-AGE DONBURI, 40
AUTUMN HARVEST RICE, 62

baby sardine, 30, 77
BABY SARDINE DONBURI, 30
BACON AND EGG DONBURI, 73
bean vermicelli, 57
Beef
  curried, 55
  ground, 31, 38
  Gyu-don, 24
  sukiyaki, 39
  with asparagus, 48
  with assorted vegetables, 56
  with garlic, 49
  with onion, 50
  with tofu, 38
  with vegetables, 26
BEEF AND ASPARAGUS DONBURI, 48
BEEF AND ONION DONBURI, 50
BEEF AND VEGETABLE DONBURI, 26
BEEF BOWL, 24
BIBIMBUP, 56
black fungus, 41, 75
BUTTERED SCALLOP DONBURI, 83

CARROT RICE, 72
CELERY AND PICKLE DONBURI, 79
CHEESY SQUID DONBURI, 43
Chicken
  ground, 40, 60, 65
  fried, 41
  spicy, 57
  teriyaki, 37
  with atsu-age, 40
  with cucumber, 33
  with egg, 21
  with mushrooms, 42
  yakitori, 35

CHICKEN-AND-EGG DONBURI, 21
CHICKEN SALAD DONBURI, 33
CHICKEN TERIYAKI DONBURI, 37
chirimenjako, 30, 77
CLAM AND EGG DONBURI, 27
CLAM DONBURI, 87
CODFISH OYAKO DONBURI, 19
COD ROE DONBURI, 77
CORNED BEEF AND POTATO DONBURI, 64
CRAB OYAKO-DONBURI, 19
CRISP BACON DONBURI, 29
CURRIED SARDINE DONBURI, 84
CURRIED TOFU DONBURI, 44
CURRY DONBURI, 55

dashimaki tamago, 16
dembu, 73
DIM SUM (SIU MAI) DONBURI, 74

eel, 25, 61
EEL OMELET DONBURI, 61
Egg
  omelet, 71
  scrambled, 35, 60, 64, 71, 72
  with bacon, 73
  with beef, 26, 31
  with chicken, 21
  with clam, 27
  with crab meat, 59
  with eel, 61
  with garlic chives, 51
  with gobo, 26
  with mushrooms, 65
  with pork cutlet, 22
  with siu mai, 74
  with tuna, 71
EGG FU YUNG DONBURI, 59
EGGPLANT WITH MISO DONBURI, 68
enokidake mushroom →see Mushrooms

Fish →see Seafood
FISH AND YAM DONBURI, 65
fish cake →see kamaboko
FISH CAKE DONBURI, 79

Fish eggs
  cod roe, 14, 19, 38
  crab eggs, 19
  salmon roe, 11, 18
FISHERMEN'S CLAM DONBURI, 21
FLAKED SALMON DONBURI, 78
FRIED CHICKEN DONBURI, 41
FRIED EGGPLANT DONBURI, 65
FRIED PRAWN DONBURI, 22
FRIED RICE WITH PICKLED PLUMS, 77
FRIED SCALLOP DONBURI, 37

GARLIC OCTOPUS DONBURI, 57
GARLIC OMELET DONBURI, 51
GARLIC SCALLOP DONBURI, 86
GARLIC STEAK DONBURI, 49
GINGER OYSTER DONBURI, 45
GINGER PORK DONBURI, 50
ginger root, 15, 21, 34, 37, 40, 45, 47, 48, 50, 52, 54, 55, 56, 57, 59, 60, 65, 66, 68, 75, 83
gomokuzushi-no-moto, 73
GRILLED SQUID DONBURI, 66
Gyu-don, 24

ikura, 11, 18

kabayaki, 25, 88
kamaboko, 16, 60, 72, 79
Katsu-don, 22, 23
kezuribushi, 29, 32
kimchee, 47
kinome, 25, 30, 77
kochu jang, 53, 56,
konnyaku, 78, 79

MAGURO SASHIMI DONBURI, 12
MAPO DONBURI, 38
MARINATED SQUID DONBURI, 14
MASHED MAGURO DONBURI, 13
MAYONNAISE PORK DONBURI, 51
mentaiko, 14
miso, 23, 49, 56, 68, 69
mitsuba, 11, 17, 21, 22, 27, 37, 60, 62, 78, 88

MIXED *MAGURO* DONBURI, 12
MIXED SALMON DONBURI, 67
MIXED SEAFOOD DONBURI, 75
MIXED *TEMPURA* DONBURI, 43
MOLOHAIRE DONBURI, 32
MOON AND MUSHROOM DONBURI, 65
MUSHROOM AND OKRA DONBURI, 32
MUSHROOM DONBURI, 63
Mushrooms
  dried black fungus, 41, 75
  enokidake, 65
  nameko, 32
  nametake, 32
  shiitake, 26, 34, 39, 41, 54, 59, 63, 77, 85
  shimeji, 42, 62, 63, 65
myoga, 78

nakaochi, 13
NAKAOCHI DONBURI, 13
NAMEKO DONBURI, 32
nameko mushroom →see Mushrooms
nametake →see Mushrooms
natto →see Soybean products
NATTO DONBURI, 68
Negitoro-don, 13
nikujaga, 67
nori seaweed, 11, 12, 14, 15, 17, 32, 56, 65, 67, 81, 87

OCTOPUS DONBURI, 15
OIL SARDINE DONBURI, 83
OMELET DONBURI, 71
Oyako-don, 21

PEPPER AND SARDINE DONBURI, 77
PEPPER SHELLFISH DONBURI, 62
pickled ginger, 24, 29, 60
Pickles
  assorted, 81
  kimchee, 47
  nozawana, 81
  shiba-zuke, 81
  Sichuan pickles, 54, 79
  takuan, 81

Pork
  cutlet, 22
  cutlet with *miso* sauce, 23
  ground, 71, 80
  roasted, 69
  spicy ground meat, 48
  spicy *shabushabu*, 53
  with bean vermicelli, 57
  with cabbage, 47
  with ginger, 50
  with kimchee, 47
  with mayonnaise, 51
  with *miso*, 49
  with potatoes, 67
  with *tofu*, 56
  with vegetables, 59
PORK AND CABBAGE DONBURI, 47
PORK AND KIMCHEE DONBURI, 47
PORK AND POTATO DONBURI, 67
PORK CUTLET DONBURI, 22
PORK CUTLET DONBURI WITH *MISO* SAUCE, 23
PORK *MISO* DONBURI, 49
RICE PORRIDGE WITH SWEET POTATO, 81
ROASTED PORK DONBURI, 69

SALAD DONBURI, 80
SALMON *OYAKO* DONBUR, 18
SALMON ROE DONBURI, 11
SALMON STEAK DONBURI, 84
SASHIMI AND YAM DONBURI, 60
SAUTÉED TUNA DONBURI, 63
SCALLION DONBURI, 29
SCRAMBLED EGG DONBURI, 35
SCRAMBLED *TOFU* DONBURI, 66
Seafood
  assorted *sashimi*, 16
  baby sardine, 30, 77
  clam, 21, 27, 87
  codfish, dried 19
  cod roe, 14, 43, 48, 77
  crab, 19, 59
  dried shrimp, 54
  fresh water clams, 62

  frozen mix, 75
  horse mackerel, dried 65
  kodai sasazuke, 60
  maguro sashimi, 12, 13, 60
  octopus, 15, 52, 57
  oyster, 45
  prawn, 22, 25
  salmon , 18, 67, 79, 84, 87
  sardine, 84, 88
  sardine, canned 83
  scallop, 16, 37, 83, 86
  sea urchin, 11
  shirimp, 41, 43, 44, 53,62
  squid, 14, 15, 16, 43, 45, 48, 66
  swordfish, 85
  trough shell, 17
  tuna, canned 71
SEA URCHIN DONBURI, 11
sesame oil, 53, 54, 55, 56, 57, 66, 69, 77
sesame seeds, 11, 12, 37, 53, 56, 67, 78, 81, 84
shiitake mushroom →see Mushrooms
shimeji mushroom →see Mushrooms
shirataki, 39, 67
shiso, 13, 14, 17, 18, 19, 34, 43, 63, 65, 66, 67, 77, 83
SICHUAN PICKLE DONBURI, 54
SICHUAN SHRIMP DONBURI, 53
SOBORO DONBURI, 31
Soybean products
  abura-age, 34, 30
  atsu-age, 40
  grilled *tofu*, 39
  natto, 15, 32, 68
  tofu, 38, 44, 56, 66
SPICY CHICKEN DONBURI, 57
SPICY GROUND MEAT DONBURI, 54
SPICY PORK-*SHABUSHABU* DONBURI, 53
SPICY VERMICELLI DONBURI, 57
SPICY YAM CAKE DONBURI, 78
SPRING DONBURI, 60
SQUID AND COD ROE DONBURI, 14
SQUID AND *NATTO* DONBURI ,15
SQUID DONBURI, 48

STEWED OCTOPUS DONBURI, 52
STIR-FRIED CHICKEN AND MUSHROOM
    DONBURI, 42
sudachi citron, 15, 17
sui mai, 74
sukiyaki, 39
SUKIYAKI DONBURI, 39
SUSHI MELANGE DONBURI, 73
SWEET SOUR SHRIMP DONBURI, 41
SWEET SOUR SWORDFISH DONBURI,
    85

tarako, 19, 38, 81
TARAMO DONBURI, 38
Tekka-don, 12
TEMPURA DONBURI, 25
Ten-don, 25
TERIYAKI EEL DONBURI, 25
TERIYAKI SARDINE DONBURI, 88
toban jang, 38, 53, 54, 56, 57
tofu →see Soybean products
TOFU AND PORK DONBURI, 56
TRI-COLOR DONBURI, 60
TRI-COLOR MIXED RICE, 74
TROUGH SHELL SCALLOP DONBURI, 17
TUNA AND EGG DONBURI, 71

umeboshi, 77
Una-don, 25

Vegetables
    asparagaus, 48
    assorted, 56
    bean sprout, 56
    bell pepper, 43, 44, 51, 52, 54, 57, 77
    bok choy, 45, 66, 69
    cabbage, 47, 50
    carrot, 56, 59, 63, 72, 75, 80, 85
    celery, 79
    Chinese cabbage, 39, 59
    cucumber, 33, 57, 80
    daikon radish, 33, 41
    eggplant, 65, 68
    garlic chives, 51
    garlic shoots, 48

gobo, 26 ,27
green bean, 40, 57, 60
green pea, 31, 38, 40, 52, 59, 67, 71, 74,
    77, 85
komatsuna green, 79
long onion ,7, 23, 35, 39, 47, 48, 49, 53,
    54, 57, 59, 61, 78
molohaire, 32
nira, 38
okra, 32
onion, 21, 22, 24, 37, 43, 44, 50, 52, 55,
    63, 64, 67, 71, 74
poteto, 38, 64, 67
salad, 80
spinach, 55, 56, 86
sweet poteto, 81
winter melon, 80
yama-imo yam, 60, 65

wasabi, 11, 13, 65
wild plants, 8, 30
WILD PLANTS DONBURI, 30
WINTER MELON AND MEAT SAUCE
    DONBURI, 80

YAKITORI DONBURI, 35
yama-imo, 17, 65
yam cake, 78, 79
yam noodles, 39, 67, 71
yuzu citron, 32, 52

BASIC MEASUREMENTS

1 teaspoon (tsp) = 5 ml
1 tablespoon (Tbsp) =15 ml
1 cup = 240 ml

Weight converted from volume

Level Measurements

	1 tsp	1 Tbsp	1 cup
water, vinegar, *sake*	5 g	15 g	240 g
soy sauce, *mirin*, *miso*	6 g	18 g	288 g
salt	5 g	15 g	240 g
sugar(granulated)	3 g	9 g	144 g

Sometimes it is simpler to estimate quantities by hand/eye measurements. Here are some practical gauges for such approximate measurements:

Hand measurements of salt

1 handful = 3 Tbsp
1 fistful = 2 Tbsp
1 pinch (with 3 fingers) = ½ tsp
1 pinch (with 2 fingers) = ¼ tsp

Eye measurements of vegetables

1 medium carrot, 4"(10 cm)long = 7 oz (200 g)
1 medium Chinese cabbage = 4½ lb (2 kg)
1 Japanese-type cucumber = 3½ oz (100 g)
1 Japanese-type eggplant = 3½ oz (100g)
1 medium turnip = 2 oz (60g)
1 thumb-size ginger root = ⅓ oz (10 g)

Converting from U.S. customary system

●Liquid Measures
1 cup = 16Tbsp = 8 oz =236 ml (240 ml)

●Weights
grams × 0.035 = ounces
ounces × 28.35 = grams

●Linear Measures
inches × 2.54 = centimeters
centimeters × 0.39 = inches

●Temperatures
$C = (F - 32) \times \frac{5}{9}$

$F = \dfrac{C \times 9}{5} + 32$

C = Celsius
F = Fahrenheit

Deep-frying oil temperatures
300°F−330°F(150°C−165°C) = low
340°F−350°F(170°C−175°C) = moderate
350°F−360°F(175°C−180°C) = high

ACKNOWLEDGMENTS

Cooking Staff : Shitsuko Watanabe
Naoko Kinoshita
Photographer : Tomohisa Tamura
Translator : Yoko Ishiguro
Project Editor : DeauVille
English Editor: Mieko Baba